COMMANDING EXCELLENCE IN MARKETING CAMPAIGNS

In the fiercely competitive world of marketing, there is no room for half-measures. *Step-by-Step Strategies for Creating Effective Marketing Campaigns* is not a guide for the faint-hearted. It is a decisive, no-nonsense manual designed for those who are committed to mastering the craft of impactful marketing.

This book is for professionals who understand that success in marketing is not accidental. It requires meticulous planning, strategic thinking, and relentless execution. We will delve deep into the core elements of campaign creation with precision, aiming to equip you with the tools necessary to dominate your market.

Throughout these pages, we will cover every essential aspect of developing a high-caliber marketing campaign—from conducting thorough market research to crafting messages that cut through the noise. You will learn to identify key performance indicators, optimize strategies for maximum impact, and analyze results with a critical eye.

Expect rigorous insights and practical strategies. This is not a handbook of fluffy theories but a resource grounded in real-world application. Each chapter is designed to challenge you to elevate your approach, demanding both discipline and creativity in equal measure.

By the end of this book, you will not only understand what it takes to create effective marketing campaigns—you will be equipped to execute them with authority and precision. Prepare to transform your marketing strategies into instruments of decisive success.

Welcome to the definitive guide for those who aim to lead rather than follow.

CHAPTER 1: INTRODUCTION TO MARKETING CAMPAIGNS

Before you can master the art of creating effective marketing campaigns, you must first understand the fundamental principles that underpin them. In this chapter, we lay the groundwork for your journey by dissecting what a marketing campaign truly entails, stripping away any misconceptions and setting the stage for strategic excellence.

Marketing campaigns are more than just promotional efforts; they are orchestrated endeavors designed to achieve specific business objectives. They demand a calculated blend of creativity, strategy, and execution. To excel, you must grasp not only the mechanics of campaign development but also the critical thinking required to drive results.

We will begin by defining the core elements of a marketing campaign, exploring its purpose, and understanding its role within the broader marketing strategy. This chapter will provide you with a clear framework for analyzing and creating campaigns that are both coherent and impactful.

Expect a rigorous examination of campaign components, including target audience identification, objective setting, and the strategic alignment of messaging. By the end of this chapter, you will have a solid foundation upon which to build more complex strategies, fully equipped to tackle the challenges and opportunities that lie ahead.

Prepare to engage with the fundamental concepts that will shape your approach to marketing campaigns. This is the starting point of your transformation into a strategic marketing leader.

DEFINITION, PURPOSE, AND IMPORTANCE IN THE DIGITAL AGE

A marketing campaign is a coordinated series of activities designed to achieve specific business objectives through targeted communication and promotional strategies. It involves a deliberate and systematic approach to delivering a unified message across multiple channels with the aim of engaging a defined audience. At its core, a marketing campaign integrates various tactics—such as advertising, content creation, and social media outreach—into a cohesive plan that drives measurable results.

Purpose

The primary purpose of a marketing campaign is to influence consumer behavior in a way that aligns with business goals. Whether the objective is to increase brand awareness, drive sales, generate leads, or foster customer loyalty, a well-executed campaign serves as a strategic tool to achieve these ends. It provides a structured approach to addressing market opportunities and challenges, ensuring that efforts are proactive and strategically aligned.

Importance in the Digital Age

In today's digital landscape, the importance of marketing campaigns is amplified. The rapid evolution of technology and the proliferation of digital channels have transformed how businesses interact with consumers. The digital age demands precision, agility, and innovation in marketing efforts:

1. **Targeted Reach**: Digital tools and platforms enable highly targeted marketing efforts. Campaigns can be tailored to specific demographics, interests, and behaviors, ensuring that your message reaches the right audience with maximum efficiency.

2. **Data-Driven Decisions**: Digital marketing campaigns are driven by data. Advanced analytics and tracking tools allow for real-time performance monitoring and insights, enabling refinement of strategies based on actual results rather than assumptions.

3. **Enhanced Engagement**: The digital age has transformed consumer expectations. Campaigns must not only reach audiences but also engage them in meaningful ways. Interactive content, personalized messaging, and multi-channel strategies are essential for capturing and retaining attention.

4. **Competitive Edge**: In a crowded digital marketplace, a well-executed marketing campaign can differentiate your brand from competitors. It allows you to showcase your unique value proposition and establish a distinct presence in the minds of consumers.

5. **Scalability and Adaptability**: Digital campaigns offer scalability and flexibility. Whether launching a global initiative or a local promotion, digital channels provide the tools to scale efforts up or down as needed, adapting to changing market conditions and consumer preferences.

TYPES OF MARKETING CAMPAIGNS: DIGITAL, TRADITIONAL, HYBRID, AND INTEGRATED CAMPAIGNS

Digital Campaigns

Digital campaigns leverage online platforms and technologies to reach and engage audiences. These campaigns use various digital channels, such as social media, search engines, email, and websites, to deliver targeted messages and promotions. Key components of digital campaigns include:

- **Social Media Advertising**: Utilizing platforms like Facebook, Instagram, and LinkedIn to promote products or services through targeted ads.

- **Search Engine Marketing (SEM)**: Employing strategies such as pay-per-click (PPC) advertising to increase visibility on search engine results pages (SERPs).

- **Email Marketing**: Sending personalized messages to subscribers to drive engagement and conversions.

- **Content Marketing**: Creating and distributing valuable content to attract and retain a clearly defined audience.

Digital campaigns are valued for their precision, scalability, and the ability to track performance in real-time.

Traditional Campaigns

Traditional marketing campaigns rely on offline channels to reach consumers. These methods have been foundational to marketing for decades and include:

- **Television and Radio Advertising**: Reaching broad audiences through commercial spots on TV and radio.

- **Print Advertising**: Utilizing newspapers, magazines, brochures, and other printed materials for promotion.

- **Outdoor Advertising**: Employing billboards, transit ads, and posters to capture attention in public spaces.

- **Direct Mail**: Sending physical promotional materials, such as postcards and catalogs, directly to consumers' mailboxes.

Despite the rise of digital marketing, traditional campaigns remain effective for reaching specific demographics and creating brand awareness on a large scale.

Hybrid Campaigns

Hybrid campaigns combine elements of both digital and traditional marketing to create a cohesive strategy that leverages the strengths of each. These campaigns aim to maximize reach and engagement by integrating offline and online efforts. Examples of hybrid campaigns include:

- **Event Promotion**: Using traditional methods like posters and direct mail to promote an event, while simultaneously leveraging digital channels for online registration and engagement.

- **Cross-Channel Advertising**: Running TV ads with corresponding digital ads that drive viewers to online content or offers.

- **Integrated Promotions**: Combining in-store promotions with online campaigns to create a unified customer experience.

Hybrid campaigns allow marketers to reach audiences through multiple touchpoints, enhancing overall effectiveness.

Integrated Campaigns

Integrated marketing campaigns take a holistic approach by ensuring consistency across all marketing channels and touchpoints. The goal is to create a unified brand experience that resonates with the target audience. Key characteristics include:

- **Consistent Messaging**: Maintaining a cohesive message and visual identity across all channels.

- **Coordinated Strategies**: Aligning digital, traditional, and hybrid efforts to reinforce the campaign's objectives.

- **Cross-Channel Synergy**: Utilizing each channel to complement and amplify the others, creating a seamless consumer journey.

Integrated campaigns are essential for building a strong brand presence and delivering a coherent experience that enhances customer engagement and loyalty.

Each type of campaign offers distinct advantages, and selecting the right approach depends on your specific goals, target audience, and available resources.

SETTING CAMPAIGN GOALS: IDENTIFYING OBJECTIVES, KPIS, AND DESIRED OUTCOMES

Identifying Objectives

Before launching any marketing campaign, it is crucial to establish clear and actionable objectives. These objectives define what you aim to achieve and provide direction for the campaign. Effective objectives are specific, measurable, attainable, relevant, and time-bound (SMART). Here are key steps to identifying your objectives:

- **Define Business Goals**: Align your campaign objectives with broader business goals, such as increasing revenue, expanding market share, or improving brand awareness.

- **Understand Target Audience Needs**: Consider what your target audience values and how the campaign can address their needs or solve their problems.

- **Determine Scope and Scale**: Decide on the scope of your campaign, including geographic reach and target segments, to ensure objectives are realistic and achievable.

Common objectives for marketing campaigns include driving sales, generating leads, boosting website traffic, enhancing customer engagement, and building brand loyalty.

Establishing Key Performance Indicators (KPIs)

Key Performance Indicators (KPIs) are metrics used to evaluate the success of your campaign in achieving its objectives. KPIs provide measurable data that helps assess performance and inform decision-making. When setting KPIs:

- **Align with Objectives**: Ensure KPIs are directly related to your campaign objectives. For instance, if your goal is to increase sales, relevant KPIs might include conversion rate and revenue generated.

- **Select Relevant Metrics**: Choose metrics that accurately reflect performance. For digital campaigns, KPIs might include click-through rates, cost per acquisition, and engagement rates. For traditional campaigns, consider metrics like reach, frequency, and response rates.

- **Set Benchmarks**: Establish benchmarks or targets for each KPI to gauge performance. These benchmarks can be based on historical data, industry standards, or competitor analysis.

Effective KPIs help track progress and measure the impact of your campaign, allowing for adjustments and optimization.

Determining Desired Outcomes

Desired outcomes represent the specific results you expect to achieve from your campaign. They provide a clear picture of what success looks like and help guide the execution and evaluation of your efforts. To determine desired outcomes:

- **Specify Results**: Clearly define what success means for your campaign. This could involve achieving a certain number of conversions, generating a specific amount of revenue, or reaching a particular audience segment.

- **Quantify Goals**: Set numerical targets for your desired outcomes to facilitate measurement and comparison. For example, if your objective is to increase brand awareness, desired outcomes might include reaching a certain number of impressions or social media shares.

- **Consider Timeframes**: Establish timeframes for achieving your outcomes. This helps in setting realistic expectations and allows for timely assessment of campaign effectiveness.

By identifying clear objectives, establishing relevant KPIs, and defining desired outcomes, you set a solid foundation for developing and executing a successful marketing campaign.

CHAPTER 2: MARKET RESEARCH AND AUDIENCE ANALYSIS

Market research and audience analysis are the cornerstones of a successful marketing campaign. In Chapter 2, we delve into the critical process of gathering and interpreting data to inform your campaign strategy. This chapter equips you with the essential skills to understand your market landscape and identify your target audience with precision.

Effective market research involves systematically collecting and analyzing data about market trends, competitors, and consumer behavior. Coupled with audience analysis, this process provides the insights needed to tailor your campaign to meet specific needs and preferences. You will learn how to leverage both qualitative and quantitative research methods to build a comprehensive understanding of your market environment.

We will explore techniques for gathering actionable data, including surveys, focus groups, and competitive analysis, and discuss how to apply these insights to refine your campaign strategy. Additionally, you will gain tools for segmenting your audience, identifying key personas, and understanding their motivations and pain points.

By the end of this chapter, you will have a solid foundation in market research and audience analysis, enabling you to make informed decisions and develop targeted marketing strategies that resonate with your audience and drive meaningful results.

CONDUCTING MARKET RESEARCH: TECHNIQUES AND TOOLS FOR UNDERSTANDING MARKET TRENDS AND CONSUMER BEHAVIOR

Techniques for Market Research

1. **Surveys and Questionnaires**

   o **Purpose**: Collect quantitative data directly from consumers regarding their preferences, behaviors, and opinions.

   o **Execution**: Design clear and concise questions that address specific areas of interest. Use online platforms like SurveyMonkey or Google Forms to distribute surveys and gather responses efficiently.

   o **Advantages**: Provides measurable insights into consumer attitudes and market trends, allowing for statistical analysis.

2. **Focus Groups**

   o **Purpose**: Obtain qualitative insights through in-depth discussions with a small group of participants.

   o **Execution**: Organize sessions with a diverse group of participants relevant to your target market. Facilitate discussions to explore attitudes, perceptions, and experiences related to your product or service.

   o **Advantages**: Offers detailed feedback and deeper understanding of consumer motivations and perceptions.

3. **Interviews**

- Purpose: Gain in-depth insights through one-on-one interactions with individuals who have expertise or influence in your market.

- Execution: Conduct structured or semi-structured interviews with industry experts, customers, or stakeholders. Use both open-ended and specific questions to explore detailed responses.

- Advantages: Provides comprehensive information and personal perspectives that can reveal underlying trends and issues.

4. **Competitive Analysis**

- Purpose: Assess the strengths and weaknesses of your competitors to identify market opportunities and threats.

- Execution: Analyze competitors' products, pricing, marketing strategies, and customer reviews. Tools like SEMrush and Ahrefs can help evaluate competitors' online presence and performance.

- Advantages: Helps in understanding competitive dynamics and positioning your campaign to leverage market gaps.

5. **Market Segmentation**

- Purpose: Divide the market into distinct segments based on demographics, psychographics, and behavior to tailor your marketing efforts.

- Execution: Use demographic data (age, gender, income) and psychographic data (interests, lifestyle) to segment your audience. Apply segmentation tools and techniques to identify specific target groups.

  o **Advantages**: Allows for more personalized and targeted marketing strategies, enhancing relevance and engagement.

Tools for Market Research

1. **Google Trends**

  o **Purpose**: Analyze search trends and patterns to gauge interest in specific topics or keywords over time.

  o **Features**: Provides insights into search volume, regional interest, and related queries.

2. **Social Media Analytics**

  o **Purpose**: Monitor and analyze social media platforms for trends, sentiment, and engagement.

  o **Tools**: Platforms like Hootsuite, Sprout Social, and Brandwatch offer analytics for tracking brand mentions, sentiment analysis, and audience insights.

3. **CRM Systems**

  o **Purpose**: Manage customer data and interactions to gain insights into customer behavior and preferences.

  o **Tools**: Salesforce, HubSpot, and Zoho CRM provide data on customer interactions, purchasing behavior, and engagement.

4. **Industry Reports and Market Research Databases**

   o **Purpose**: Access comprehensive reports and data on market trends, industry forecasts, and consumer behavior.

   o **Sources**: Reports from Nielsen, Statista, and IBISWorld offer valuable market insights and statistics.

5. **Heatmaps and User Behavior Analytics**

   o **Purpose**: Analyze how users interact with your website or digital assets.

   o **Tools**: Tools like Hotjar and Crazy Egg provide visual insights into user behavior, such as click patterns and scroll depth.

By employing these techniques and tools, you can gain a thorough understanding of market trends and consumer behavior, providing a solid foundation for developing targeted and effective marketing strategies.

IDENTIFYING TARGET AUDIENCE: SEGMENTATION, BUYER PERSONAS, AND DEMOGRAPHIC ANALYSIS

Segmentation

Segmentation involves dividing the broader market into distinct groups of consumers who share similar characteristics, needs, or behaviors. This process allows for more targeted and effective marketing strategies. Key segmentation approaches include:

1. **Demographic Segmentation**

   o **Criteria**: Age, gender, income, education, occupation, and family status.

   o **Purpose**: Identifies groups based on measurable attributes, helping to tailor messages and offers to specific demographic profiles.

   o **Example**: Marketing luxury goods to high-income earners or targeting educational products to students and parents.

2. **Geographic Segmentation**

   o **Criteria**: Location, such as country, region, city, or neighborhood.

   o **Purpose**: Addresses location-specific needs and preferences, allowing for localized marketing efforts.

   o **Example**: Promoting weather-related products in regions experiencing extreme weather conditions.

3. **Psychographic Segmentation**

- o **Criteria**: Lifestyle, values, interests, and attitudes.

- o **Purpose**: Understands the motivations and preferences that drive consumer behavior, enabling the creation of more personalized marketing messages.

- o **Example**: Targeting eco-friendly products to consumers who prioritize sustainability.

4. **Behavioral Segmentation**

- o **Criteria**: Purchasing behavior, usage rate, brand loyalty, and decision-making patterns.

- o **Purpose**: Focuses on how consumers interact with products or services, identifying patterns that can inform marketing strategies.

- o **Example**: Offering discounts to frequent buyers or targeting users who have shown interest in a product category.

Buyer Personas

Buyer personas are detailed, semi-fictional representations of your ideal customers based on research and data. They provide a clear picture of your target audience, helping to align marketing strategies with customer needs and preferences. To create effective buyer personas:

1. **Conduct Research**

- o **Methods**: Use surveys, interviews, and customer data to gather information about your audience's demographics, behaviors, and preferences.

- o **Sources**: Analyze CRM data, social media insights, and industry reports to build a comprehensive understanding of your target audience.

2. **Define Persona Characteristics**

   - o **Attributes**: Include demographic details (age, gender, income), psychographic information (interests, values), and behavioral traits (buying habits, brand loyalty).

   - o **Example**: A buyer persona might be "Sarah, 35, a health-conscious mother who values organic products and shops online frequently."

3. **Develop Persona Profiles**

   - o **Details**: Create detailed profiles for each persona, including name, background, goals, challenges, and purchasing motivations.

   - o **Usage**: Use these profiles to guide content creation, messaging, and campaign strategies to better address the needs and preferences of each persona.

Demographic Analysis

Demographic analysis involves studying the statistical characteristics of a population to gain insights into their needs and behaviors. This analysis helps in understanding the composition and trends within your target audience. Key steps include:

1. **Collect Demographic Data**

- ○ **Sources**: Gather data from market research reports, government statistics, and customer surveys.

- ○ **Metrics**: Analyze attributes such as age distribution, gender ratios, income levels, education, and occupation.

2. **Analyze Trends and Patterns**

   - ○ **Trends**: Identify emerging trends and shifts in demographic data that may impact consumer behavior and preferences.

   - ○ **Patterns**: Look for patterns in how different demographic groups respond to marketing efforts and products.

3. **Apply Insights to Marketing Strategies**

   - ○ **Tailoring**: Adjust your marketing strategies and messages to align with the demographic characteristics of your target audience.

   - ○ **Segmentation**: Use demographic insights to refine market segmentation and ensure your campaigns are relevant to specific groups.

By utilizing segmentation, developing detailed buyer personas, and conducting thorough demographic analysis, you can effectively identify and understand your target audience. This understanding enables you to create targeted marketing strategies that resonate with your audience and drive meaningful engagement.

COMPETITOR ANALYSIS: TOOLS AND METHODS FOR ANALYZING COMPETITORS AND MARKET POSITIONING

Tools for Competitor Analysis

1. **Competitive Intelligence Platforms**

   - **SEMrush**: Provides comprehensive data on competitors' digital marketing strategies, including keywords, backlinks, and advertising tactics. Useful for understanding SEO and PPC performance.

   - **Ahrefs**: Offers detailed insights into competitors' link profiles, keyword rankings, and content strategies. Ideal for identifying SEO opportunities and weaknesses.

   - **SpyFu**: Analyzes competitors' keywords and ad campaigns, providing insights into their PPC strategies and budget allocations.

2. **Social Media Monitoring Tools**

   - **Hootsuite**: Allows for tracking and analyzing competitors' social media activities, engagement rates, and content performance. Helps identify trends and benchmarks.

   - **Brandwatch**: Provides in-depth analysis of brand mentions, sentiment, and social media conversations, offering insights into competitors' online presence and reputation.

   - **Sprout Social**: Offers analytics on competitors' social media performance, including follower growth, engagement metrics, and content strategies.

3. **Website Analysis Tools**

   o **SimilarWeb**: Delivers insights into competitors' website traffic, sources, and user behavior. Helps assess traffic volume and online presence.

   o **Alexa**: Provides data on website rankings, audience demographics, and engagement metrics, enabling comparisons with competitors.

   o **BuiltWith**: Analyzes competitors' technology stack and web infrastructure, offering insights into their digital tools and platforms.

4. **Market Research Databases**

   o **Statista**: Offers access to a wide range of industry statistics, market reports, and competitor data, useful for understanding market trends and positioning.

   o **IBISWorld**: Provides detailed industry reports and competitor analysis, including market share, competitive landscape, and industry performance.

Methods for Competitor Analysis

1. **SWOT Analysis**

   o **Purpose**: Evaluates competitors' strengths, weaknesses, opportunities, and threats to understand their market positioning and strategic advantages.

   o **Execution**: Analyze each competitor's capabilities, market performance, and potential risks. Use this analysis to identify areas where your business can differentiate itself.

2. **Benchmarking**

   o **Purpose**: Compares your business's performance metrics against those of competitors to identify best practices and performance gaps.

   o **Execution**: Collect data on key performance indicators (KPIs) such as market share, customer satisfaction, and financial performance. Compare these metrics with competitors to gauge relative performance.

3. **Competitor Profiling**

   o **Purpose**: Develop detailed profiles of key competitors to understand their market strategies, target audiences, and business models.

   o **Execution**: Gather information on competitors' product offerings, pricing strategies, marketing tactics, and customer feedback. Create profiles that highlight their market position and strategic focus.

4. **Market Positioning Analysis**

   o **Purpose**: Assess how competitors are positioned in the market relative to your business, including their unique selling propositions (USPs) and brand positioning.

   o **Execution**: Analyze competitors' branding, messaging, and customer value propositions. Identify their strengths and weaknesses in positioning and use this information to refine your own market strategy.

5. **Competitive Benchmarking**

   o **Purpose**: Compares specific aspects of your business with those of competitors to identify performance gaps and opportunities for improvement.

   o **Execution**: Focus on specific elements such as customer service, product features, or pricing strategies. Evaluate how your offerings compare and identify areas for enhancement.

By utilizing these tools and methods, you can gain a comprehensive understanding of your competitors and their market positioning. This analysis will inform your strategic decisions, helping you to differentiate your business, capitalize on market opportunities, and strengthen your competitive edge.

CHAPTER 3: DEVELOPING A CAMPAIGN STRATEGY

A campaign strategy is the blueprint for translating your marketing objectives into actionable plans. In Chapter 3, we dive into the intricate process of crafting a strategy that will steer your campaign from conception to execution with precision and purpose.

Developing a robust campaign strategy requires more than just creative ideas; it demands a deep understanding of your target audience, a clear articulation of your campaign's goals, and a detailed plan for how to achieve them. This chapter will guide you through each essential component of a successful campaign strategy, ensuring that every decision and action is aligned with your overarching objectives.

We will cover critical elements such as defining your target audience with accuracy, selecting the most effective channels for your message, and designing a compelling value proposition. Additionally, you will learn how to allocate resources efficiently and anticipate potential challenges.

By the end of this chapter, you will have the tools and insights needed to develop a strategic framework that not only directs your campaign but also maximizes its impact. Prepare to turn your campaign goals into a structured plan of action that drives results and sets the stage for a successful execution.

CRAFTING A VALUE PROPOSITION: CREATING A UNIQUE SELLING POINT (USP) THAT RESONATES WITH YOUR AUDIENCE

Understanding the Value Proposition

A value proposition is a clear statement that defines the unique benefits and value your product or service offers to your target audience. It communicates why customers should choose your offering over competitors', focusing on the specific problems you solve and the advantages you provide. Crafting an effective value proposition is crucial for differentiating your brand and compelling your audience to take action.

Steps to Crafting a Value Proposition

1. **Identify Customer Pain Points and Needs**

   o **Research**: Conduct market research to understand the challenges and needs of your target audience. Use surveys, interviews, and feedback to gather insights.

   o **Analysis**: Analyze common problems and desires that your product or service addresses. Identify gaps in the market that your offering can fill.

2. **Define Your Unique Selling Points (USPs)**

   o **Features and Benefits**: List the key features of your product or service and the benefits they provide. Focus on what makes your offering distinct from competitors'.

   o **Competitive Edge**: Identify your competitive advantages, such as superior quality, unique technology, or exceptional customer service.

Highlight aspects that set you apart in the market.

3. **Craft a Clear and Compelling Statement**

   o **Format**: Develop a concise statement that communicates the core value of your offering. The statement should be easy to understand and memorable.

   o **Components**: Include the following elements:

      ▪ **Target Audience**: Specify who your ideal customers are.

      ▪ **Problem Solved**: Clearly state the problem or need your offering addresses.

      ▪ **Unique Benefits**: Highlight the unique benefits and features that differentiate your product or service.

      ▪ **Value Delivered**: Convey the overall value and impact your offering provides to customers.

4. **Test and Refine Your Value Proposition**

   o **Feedback**: Gather feedback from your target audience to evaluate the effectiveness of your value proposition. Test different versions to see which resonates best.

   o **Iteration**: Refine your statement based on feedback and performance metrics. Ensure it aligns with customer expectations and market demands.

Examples of Effective Value Propositions

1. **Apple's iPhone**

   o **Value Proposition**: "The iPhone combines cutting-edge technology with a sleek design and user-friendly experience. It delivers unparalleled performance and integrates seamlessly with Apple's ecosystem."

   o **Components**: Targets tech-savvy consumers, solves the need for a powerful and stylish smartphone, emphasizes superior design and integration.

2. **Slack**

   o **Value Proposition**: "Slack is a collaboration hub that connects your work with the people you work with. It streamlines communication, boosts productivity, and integrates with tools you already use."

   o **Components**: Targets teams and organizations, addresses communication challenges, highlights productivity improvements and integration.

Integrating Your Value Proposition into Your Campaign

1. **Consistency Across Channels**

   o **Messaging**: Ensure your value proposition is consistently communicated across all marketing channels, including your website, social media, and advertising materials.

   o **Brand Voice**: Maintain a consistent tone and style that reflects your brand's personality and values.

2. **Customer-Centric Approach**

- Alignment: Align your value proposition with the needs and preferences of your target audience. Use it to address their specific pain points and demonstrate how your offering meets their needs.

3. **Highlighting in Campaign Elements**

   - **Content**: Incorporate your value proposition into key campaign elements such as headlines, calls-to-action, and promotional materials. Use it to capture attention and drive engagement.

Crafting a compelling value proposition is essential for creating a unique selling point that resonates with your audience. By clearly defining what sets you apart and how you address customer needs, you can effectively differentiate your brand and drive meaningful connections with your target market.

CHOOSING MARKETING CHANNELS: EVALUATING AND SELECTING THE RIGHT CHANNELS (SOCIAL MEDIA, EMAIL, PPC, ETC.)

Evaluating Marketing Channels

Selecting the right marketing channels is crucial for reaching your target audience effectively and maximizing the impact of your campaign. Each channel has its strengths and can be leveraged in different ways depending on your goals, audience, and budget. Here's how to evaluate and choose the most suitable channels for your campaign:

1. **Understand Your Audience**

   o **Research**: Use market research and audience analysis to determine where your target audience spends their time and how they prefer to receive information.

   o **Behavior**: Analyze behavioral patterns to identify which channels they engage with most frequently, whether it's social media, email, search engines, or other platforms.

2. **Define Your Goals**

   o **Objectives**: Align your choice of channels with your campaign objectives, whether it's brand awareness, lead generation, customer engagement, or sales conversion.

   o **Metrics**: Determine the key performance indicators (KPIs) for each channel to measure success and ensure it supports your campaign goals.

Types of Marketing Channels

1. **Social Media**

   o **Overview**: Platforms like Facebook, Instagram, Twitter, LinkedIn, and TikTok offer diverse opportunities for engaging with audiences through organic content and paid ads.

   o **Strengths**: High engagement potential, real-time interaction, targeted advertising options, and extensive reach.

   o **Considerations**: Choose platforms based on your audience demographics and campaign objectives. For example, Instagram and TikTok are ideal for visually-driven content and younger audiences, while LinkedIn is better for B2B marketing and professional networking.

2. **Email Marketing**

   o **Overview**: Involves sending targeted messages directly to a subscriber's inbox. Common uses include newsletters, promotional offers, and personalized updates.

   o **Strengths**: Direct communication with a captive audience, high ROI, and the ability to personalize and segment messages.

   o **Considerations**: Build and maintain a quality email list, and ensure compliance with regulations like GDPR and CAN-SPAM. Use A/B testing to optimize subject lines, content, and calls-to-action.

3. **Pay-Per-Click (PPC) Advertising**

   o **Overview**: Paid search ads (e.g., Google Ads) and display ads appear on search engines and websites, targeting users based on keywords and demographics.

- o **Strengths**: Immediate visibility, precise targeting, measurable results, and the ability to control budget and bids.

- o **Considerations**: Conduct keyword research to identify high-performing terms, set clear goals for click-through rates (CTR) and conversion rates, and continuously optimize ad performance.

4. **Content Marketing**

- o **Overview**: Involves creating and distributing valuable content to attract and engage your target audience. This can include blog posts, videos, infographics, and eBooks.

- o **Strengths**: Builds brand authority, drives organic traffic, and nurtures customer relationships through informative and valuable content.

- o **Considerations**: Develop a content strategy that aligns with audience interests and needs, and use SEO best practices to enhance visibility and reach.

5. **Influencer Marketing**

- o **Overview**: Partners with individuals who have a significant following and influence in your industry to promote your brand or product.

- o **Strengths**: Leverages the trust and credibility of influencers to reach a targeted audience and boost brand awareness.

- o **Considerations**: Choose influencers whose audience aligns with your target market, and establish clear goals and metrics for the partnership.

6. **Affiliate Marketing**

   - o **Overview**: Involves partnering with affiliates who promote your products or services in exchange for a commission on sales or leads generated.

   - o **Strengths**: Expands reach through a network of affiliates, with performance-based payment models that reduce risk.

   - o **Considerations**: Recruit reputable affiliates, set clear terms and commission structures, and track performance to ensure effectiveness.

Selecting the Right Channels

1. **Match Channels to Audience Preferences**

   - o **Alignment**: Choose channels that align with where your audience is most active and responsive. Consider their habits, preferences, and the type of content they engage with.

2. **Evaluate Cost and ROI**

   - o **Budget**: Assess the cost of each channel and its potential return on investment (ROI). Allocate resources to channels that offer the best balance of cost and performance.

3. **Integrate Across Channels**

   - o **Consistency**: Ensure your messaging is consistent across all chosen channels. Create a cohesive strategy that leverages the strengths of each channel to reinforce your campaign objectives.

4. **Monitor and Adjust**

   o **Analytics**: Use analytics tools to track performance and measure the effectiveness of each channel. Adjust your strategy based on data insights and campaign results to optimize performance.

By carefully evaluating and selecting the right marketing channels, you can effectively reach and engage your target audience, drive meaningful results, and achieve your campaign objectives.

BUDGETING AND RESOURCE ALLOCATION: ESTIMATING COSTS, ALLOCATING RESOURCES, AND MAXIMIZING ROI

Estimating Costs

1. **Identify Key Expenses**

   o **Direct Costs**: Include expenditures related to specific marketing activities such as ad spend, content creation, software tools, and media buys.

   o **Indirect Costs**: Account for overheads like salaries for marketing staff, agency fees, and administrative expenses.

2. **Estimate Costs for Each Channel**

   o **Social Media**: Costs may include paid ads, content creation, social media management tools, and influencer fees.

   o **Email Marketing**: Factor in expenses for email platforms, design, list management, and automation tools.

   o **PPC Advertising**: Include costs for ad placements, keyword bidding, and campaign management tools.

   o **Content Marketing**: Budget for content production, distribution, and SEO optimization.

   o **Influencer Marketing**: Consider fees for influencer partnerships, content creation, and campaign management.

3. **Forecast Contingency Costs**

- o **Unexpected Expenses**: Set aside a portion of your budget for unforeseen costs, such as additional ad spend or extra production needs.

- o **Flexibility**: Ensure your budget can accommodate adjustments based on campaign performance and market conditions.

Allocating Resources

1. **Determine Resource Needs**

   - o **Personnel**: Identify the team members required for each aspect of the campaign, including content creators, designers, and analysts.

   - o **Tools and Technology**: Invest in necessary tools for campaign management, analytics, and automation to streamline processes and improve efficiency.

2. **Distribute Budget Across Channels**

   - o **Prioritize Channels**: Allocate budget based on the effectiveness and potential ROI of each channel. Focus on channels that align with your target audience and campaign objectives.

   - o **Balance**: Ensure a balanced approach to avoid over-investing in one channel at the expense of others. Diversify your budget to cover various touchpoints.

3. **Monitor Resource Utilization**

   - o **Tracking**: Regularly track the allocation of resources and expenditures to ensure they align with the planned budget.

- o **Adjustment**: Reallocate resources as needed based on performance data and shifting priorities. Be prepared to adjust budgets to optimize results.

Maximizing ROI

1. **Set Clear Objectives and KPIs**

   - o **Objectives**: Define specific, measurable goals for each campaign element, such as lead generation, sales conversion, or brand awareness.

   - o **KPIs**: Identify key performance indicators (KPIs) to measure success, including cost per acquisition (CPA), return on ad spend (ROAS), and customer lifetime value (CLV).

2. **Optimize Campaign Performance**

   - o **A/B Testing**: Conduct A/B tests on various elements such as ad creatives, headlines, and targeting options to determine the most effective combinations.

   - o **Data Analysis**: Analyze performance data to identify trends, strengths, and weaknesses. Use insights to refine strategies and improve results.

3. **Implement Cost-Effective Strategies**

   - o **Leverage Free and Low-Cost Tools**: Utilize free or low-cost marketing tools for analytics, social media management, and content distribution to maximize your budget.

   - o **Repurpose Content**: Extend the value of your content by repurposing it for different formats and channels. For example, turn blog posts into social media updates or videos.

4. **Monitor and Adjust Budget Allocation**

   o **Performance Review**: Continuously review campaign performance and ROI. Adjust budgets and resource allocation based on which channels and tactics are delivering the best results.

   o **Iterative Improvement**: Make data-driven decisions to optimize budget distribution and resource usage over time, ensuring ongoing improvements in campaign efficiency and effectiveness.

By carefully estimating costs, strategically allocating resources, and focusing on maximizing ROI, you can effectively manage your marketing budget and achieve your campaign objectives. This approach ensures that your resources are utilized efficiently, delivering the best possible results for your investment.

CHAPTER 4: CONTENT CREATION AND MESSAGING

In the digital landscape, content is the cornerstone of effective marketing. It's not just about filling a space on your website or social media; it's about creating compelling narratives that resonate with your audience, drive engagement, and inspire action. Chapter 4 delves into the art and science of content creation and messaging, focusing on how to craft messages that capture attention and deliver value.

This chapter will guide you through the process of developing content that aligns with your brand's voice and objectives while addressing your audience's needs and preferences. We'll explore various content formats, from written articles and blog posts to multimedia elements like videos and infographics. You'll learn how to create content that not only communicates your value proposition effectively but also engages your audience and drives meaningful interactions.

We'll also examine the importance of messaging consistency across different platforms and how to tailor your content to different stages of the customer journey. By understanding the principles of persuasive messaging and content strategy, you'll be equipped to build a strong, cohesive brand presence that stands out in a crowded digital marketplace.

Prepare to dive deep into the strategies and best practices for creating content that not only attracts but also retains your audience, fostering lasting relationships and driving your marketing success.

CONTENT STRATEGY: DEVELOPING A CONTENT CALENDAR AND PLANNING CONTENT TYPES

Developing a Content Calendar

1. **Define Objectives and Goals**

   o **Alignment**: Ensure that your content calendar aligns with your overall marketing objectives and campaign goals. Identify what you want to achieve with your content, such as increasing brand awareness, driving traffic, or generating leads.

   o **KPIs**: Set clear key performance indicators (KPIs) to measure the success of your content, such as engagement rates, click-through rates, or conversion metrics.

2. **Audience Research and Segmentation**

   o **Identify Needs**: Understand your audience's preferences, pain points, and interests. Segment your audience based on demographics, behavior, and needs to tailor content accordingly.

   o **Personalization**: Plan content that addresses the specific needs of each audience segment, ensuring it resonates with them and drives engagement.

3. **Plan Content Themes and Topics**

   o **Themes**: Develop overarching themes that align with your brand's messaging and campaign goals. These themes will guide the creation of relevant and cohesive content.

- ○ **Topics**: Brainstorm and select specific topics under each theme that address audience interests and current trends. Ensure a mix of educational, entertaining, and promotional content.

4. **Create a Content Calendar**

- ○ **Template**: Use a content calendar template to organize your content schedule. Include columns for publication dates, content types, platforms, and responsible team members.

- ○ **Schedule**: Plan content publication dates and times based on audience engagement patterns and platform best practices. Ensure a consistent posting frequency to maintain audience engagement.

- ○ **Deadlines**: Set deadlines for content creation, review, and approval to ensure timely delivery and avoid last-minute rushes.

5. **Coordinate with Campaigns and Promotions**

- ○ **Integration**: Align your content calendar with upcoming marketing campaigns, product launches, and promotions. Plan content that supports and amplifies these initiatives.

- ○ **Cross-Channel Coordination**: Ensure that content is distributed across appropriate channels and platforms, maintaining consistency in messaging and timing.

Planning Content Types

1. **Identify Content Formats**

- **Written Content**: Includes blog posts, articles, whitepapers, and eBooks. Ideal for providing in-depth information and establishing thought leadership.

- **Visual Content**: Includes images, infographics, and charts. Useful for presenting data visually and engaging audiences through visual storytelling.

- **Video Content**: Includes tutorials, explainer videos, and live streams. Effective for capturing attention and conveying complex information in an engaging format.

- **Audio Content**: Includes podcasts and voiceovers. Useful for reaching audiences who prefer audio formats and for establishing a personal connection with listeners.

2. **Determine Content Goals**

- **Educational**: Content that informs and educates your audience about relevant topics, industry trends, and best practices.

- **Entertaining**: Content designed to engage and entertain, such as stories, humor, or interactive elements.

- **Promotional**: Content focused on driving action, such as product announcements, special offers, and calls-to-action.

3. **Create Content Guidelines**

- **Brand Voice and Tone**: Establish guidelines for maintaining a consistent brand voice and tone across all content types. Ensure that content aligns with your brand's personality and messaging.

- o **Style and Formatting**: Define standards for content formatting, including style guides, visual elements, and readability. Maintain consistency in presentation and quality.

4. **Content Distribution and Promotion**

- o **Channels**: Plan how and where content will be distributed, including social media platforms, email newsletters, and your website. Choose channels based on audience preferences and content type.

- o **Promotion**: Develop strategies for promoting content, including social media shares, influencer collaborations, and paid advertising. Ensure content reaches the intended audience and drives engagement.

5. **Monitor and Adjust**

- o **Performance Tracking**: Use analytics tools to monitor the performance of your content. Track metrics such as engagement, reach, and conversion rates to evaluate effectiveness.

- o **Feedback and Optimization**: Gather feedback from your audience and analyze performance data to make informed adjustments to your content strategy. Continuously optimize content based on insights and evolving trends.

By developing a detailed content calendar and planning diverse content types, you can create a strategic approach to content creation that supports your marketing goals and resonates with your audience. This structured approach ensures that your content remains relevant, engaging, and aligned with your overall marketing strategy.

CREATING ENGAGING CONTENT: TIPS FOR WRITING COMPELLING COPY, DESIGNING VISUALS, AND PRODUCING VIDEOS

Writing Compelling Copy

1. **Know Your Audience**

   - **Research**: Understand your audience's preferences, pain points, and motivations. Tailor your copy to address their needs and interests.

   - **Language**: Use language and tone that resonate with your target audience. Speak their language and match their level of formality.

2. **Craft a Strong Headline**

   - **Attention-Grabbing**: Create headlines that capture attention and spark curiosity. Use powerful words and address the reader's main benefit or pain point.

   - **Clarity**: Ensure your headline clearly conveys what the content is about. Avoid vague or misleading headlines that might frustrate readers.

3. **Focus on Benefits, Not Features**

   - **Value Proposition**: Highlight the benefits and value your product or service provides, rather than just listing features. Explain how it solves problems or improves the reader's life.

   - **Customer-Centric**: Frame your message from the customer's perspective. Show how your offering directly addresses their needs and desires.

4. **Use Clear and Concise Language**

   o **Simplicity**: Avoid jargon and complex language. Write in a clear, straightforward manner that is easy to understand.

   o **Brevity**: Keep your copy concise and to the point. Eliminate unnecessary words and focus on delivering your message efficiently.

5. **Incorporate Strong Calls-to-Action (CTAs)**

   o **Action-Oriented**: Use actionable language that encourages readers to take the next step, such as "Sign Up," "Learn More," or "Buy Now."

   o **Visibility**: Ensure your CTA stands out visually and is placed prominently within the content.

Designing Visuals

1. **Align with Brand Identity**

   o **Consistency**: Use colors, fonts, and design elements that align with your brand's visual identity. Ensure that all visuals reflect your brand's personality and values.

   o **Logo Placement**: Include your logo in visuals to reinforce brand recognition and maintain consistency.

2. **Create Visually Appealing Graphics**

   o **High Quality**: Use high-resolution images and graphics to ensure a professional appearance. Avoid pixelation and low-quality visuals.

- o **Simplicity**: Design clean and simple visuals that convey your message clearly. Avoid cluttered designs that can distract or confuse viewers.

3. **Utilize Effective Layout and Design Principles**

   - o **Hierarchy**: Use visual hierarchy to guide the viewer's eye through the content. Highlight key elements and ensure a logical flow of information.

   - o **Contrast and Color**: Use contrast and color strategically to make important elements stand out and enhance readability.

4. **Incorporate Infographics and Data Visualization**

   - o **Clarity**: Present complex data and information in a visually appealing and easy-to-understand format. Use charts, graphs, and diagrams to convey key points.

   - o **Engagement**: Make infographics engaging and informative, combining visuals with concise explanations to enhance understanding.

Producing Videos

1. **Plan and Script Your Content**

   - o **Storyboard**: Outline the key points and structure of your video. Create a storyboard to visualize scenes and ensure a coherent flow.

   - o **Script**: Write a clear and engaging script that conveys your message effectively. Ensure it is well-paced and aligns with your video's objectives.

2. **Focus on High Production Quality**

- o **Audio and Lighting**: Invest in good quality audio and lighting equipment. Clear sound and proper lighting are crucial for a professional-looking video.

- o **Camera Work**: Use steady camera techniques and ensure proper framing. Avoid shaky footage and distractions in the background.

3. **Keep Videos Engaging and Concise**

- o **Attention Span**: Capture the viewer's attention within the first few seconds. Keep videos concise and focused on delivering the main message quickly.

- o **Visuals and Editing**: Use engaging visuals, animations, and smooth transitions. Edit your video to remove unnecessary content and enhance overall quality.

4. **Optimize for Distribution**

- o **Format**: Export videos in formats suitable for different platforms, such as MP4 for social media and website embedding.

- o **Thumbnails and Titles**: Create eye-catching thumbnails and compelling titles to attract viewers. Ensure they accurately represent the video content.

5. **Include Clear CTAs**

- o **Action**: End your video with a clear call-to-action that directs viewers to take the next step, whether it's visiting your website, subscribing to a channel, or making a purchase.

- Placement: Place CTAs strategically within the video and in the description or overlay to maximize visibility and effectiveness.

Creating engaging content involves a thoughtful approach to writing compelling copy, designing visually appealing graphics, and producing high-quality videos. By focusing on your audience's needs, maintaining brand consistency, and utilizing effective design and production techniques, you can craft content that captures attention, drives engagement, and achieves your marketing goals.

PERSONALIZATION AND SEGMENTATION: TAILORING MESSAGES FOR DIFFERENT AUDIENCE SEGMENTS

Understanding Personalization and Segmentation

1. **Personalization**

   o **Definition**: Personalization involves creating content and messaging that are specifically tailored to individual preferences, behaviors, and characteristics. It goes beyond generic messaging to address the unique needs and interests of each audience member.

   o **Benefits**: Personalized content increases relevance, improves engagement, and enhances the likelihood of conversion by making recipients feel valued and understood.

2. **Segmentation**

   o **Definition**: Segmentation is the process of dividing your audience into distinct groups based on shared characteristics or behaviors. This allows for more targeted and effective marketing efforts.

   o **Benefits**: Segmentation helps deliver content that resonates with specific groups, improving the efficiency of your marketing campaigns and increasing the chances of achieving desired outcomes.

Steps for Effective Personalization and Segmentation

1. **Collect and Analyze Data**

- Data Sources: Gather data from various sources such as website analytics, social media interactions, CRM systems, and customer surveys. This data provides insights into audience behavior, preferences, and demographics.

- Analysis: Analyze the data to identify patterns, trends, and common characteristics. Look for correlations between customer attributes and their interactions with your brand.

2. **Define Audience Segments**

- Demographic Segmentation: Group your audience based on demographic factors such as age, gender, income, and education level. This helps tailor messages to different life stages and purchasing power.

- Behavioral Segmentation: Segment based on customer behaviors, such as purchasing habits, website activity, and engagement levels. This allows you to target users with messages that reflect their interests and actions.

- Psychographic Segmentation: Use psychographic data to categorize your audience based on personality traits, values, and lifestyle preferences. This helps create content that aligns with their motivations and attitudes.

3. **Create Targeted Content**

- Message Customization: Develop personalized messages that address the specific needs and pain points of each segment. Use language and tone that resonate with their unique characteristics.

- o **Content Relevance**: Tailor content to match the interests and preferences of each segment. For example, provide product recommendations based on past purchases or offer exclusive deals based on user behavior.

4. **Utilize Automation Tools**

   - o **Email Marketing**: Use email marketing platforms to automate personalized email campaigns. Segment your email lists and create dynamic content that adjusts based on recipient data.

   - o **Ad Campaigns**: Implement targeted ad campaigns using platforms like Google Ads and social media. Utilize audience targeting options to deliver personalized ads based on user segments.

5. **Test and Optimize**

   - o **A/B Testing**: Conduct A/B tests to compare the effectiveness of different personalized messages and content variations. Measure performance based on engagement, conversion rates, and other relevant metrics.

   - o **Feedback Loop**: Collect feedback from your audience to understand how well your personalized content is resonating. Use this feedback to refine and improve your segmentation and personalization strategies.

6. **Maintain Privacy and Compliance**

   - o **Data Protection**: Ensure that you handle customer data responsibly and comply with privacy regulations such as GDPR or CCPA.

Clearly communicate how data is used and obtain necessary consents.

- Transparency: Be transparent with your audience about the data you collect and how it is used to personalize their experience. Build trust by maintaining high standards of data privacy and security.

Implementing Personalization and Segmentation

1. **Personalized Offers and Recommendations**

   - **Product Recommendations**: Use data-driven insights to recommend products or services based on individual preferences and past behaviors. Enhance the customer experience by suggesting relevant options.

   - **Exclusive Offers**: Create exclusive promotions or discounts tailored to specific segments. Reward loyal customers or target high-value segments with special incentives.

2. **Segmented Communication Channels**

   - **Tailored Messaging**: Customize your messaging for different communication channels, such as email, social media, and website content. Ensure that messages are relevant and engaging for each segment.

   - **Channel Preferences**: Respect channel preferences by delivering content through the preferred platforms of each segment. For example, reach younger audiences through social media and older audiences via email.

By effectively personalizing and segmenting your messaging, you can create a more relevant and engaging experience for your audience. Tailoring your content to meet the specific needs and interests of different segments not only enhances the impact of your marketing efforts but also fosters stronger relationships with your customers.

CHAPTER 5: IMPLEMENTATION AND EXECUTION

Effective marketing campaigns are only as successful as their execution. While a well-crafted strategy and compelling content lay the foundation, the real impact is achieved through meticulous implementation and execution. Chapter 5 focuses on transforming your strategic plans into actionable steps and ensuring that every element of your campaign is delivered seamlessly and efficiently.

In this chapter, we will explore the essential components of campaign execution, from coordinating team efforts and managing timelines to monitoring performance and adjusting tactics. We'll dive into practical steps for deploying your campaign across various channels, ensuring that every detail aligns with your objectives and resonates with your target audience.

We will cover key topics such as project management, resource allocation, and the importance of clear communication among team members. Additionally, we'll discuss strategies for maintaining flexibility and responsiveness throughout the campaign lifecycle, allowing you to adapt to unforeseen challenges and opportunities.

By the end of this chapter, you will have a comprehensive understanding of how to effectively implement and execute your marketing campaigns, driving them from concept to reality with precision and agility.

LAUNCHING THE CAMPAIGN: STEP-BY-STEP GUIDE TO ROLLING OUT THE CAMPAIGN ACROSS SELECTED CHANNELS

1. Finalize Campaign Assets

- **Content Review**: Ensure all campaign materials, including copy, visuals, and videos, are reviewed and approved. Verify that they align with your campaign objectives and brand guidelines.

- **Quality Check**: Conduct a final quality check for accuracy, consistency, and professionalism. Test all links, check for typos, and ensure all multimedia elements function correctly.

2. Coordinate with Team Members

- **Role Assignment**: Clearly define roles and responsibilities for each team member involved in the campaign. Ensure everyone understands their tasks and deadlines.

- **Communication**: Establish a communication plan to keep the team informed about progress and any issues. Use project management tools and regular meetings to facilitate coordination.

3. Schedule and Publish Content

- **Content Calendar**: Refer to your content calendar to schedule the release of each piece of content. Ensure that timing aligns with optimal engagement periods for your target audience.

- **Platform Posting**: Use scheduling tools to automate the posting of content across different platforms. Verify that posts are set to go live at the planned times.

4. Launch Campaign Across Channels

- **Website**: Update your website with relevant campaign elements, such as landing pages, banners, and pop-ups. Ensure that the website is optimized for performance and user experience.

- **Social Media**: Begin your social media rollout by publishing posts, ads, and stories according to your schedule. Engage with your audience through comments and messages to build excitement.

- **Email Marketing**: Send out campaign-related emails, including newsletters, promotional offers, and updates. Monitor email deliverability and open rates to gauge effectiveness.

- **Paid Advertising**: Launch paid ad campaigns on platforms such as Google Ads and social media. Monitor initial performance and adjust targeting or budgets as needed.

5. Monitor Performance in Real-Time

- **Analytics Tools**: Utilize analytics tools to track key performance metrics such as engagement, clicks, conversions, and traffic. Set up real-time dashboards to monitor the campaign's progress.

- **Adjustments**: Be prepared to make real-time adjustments based on performance data. If certain elements are underperforming, tweak your strategies or content to improve results.

6. Manage and Optimize Campaign

- **Ongoing Engagement**: Continue engaging with your audience through social media, email responses, and other channels. Address any questions or feedback promptly to maintain positive interactions.

- **Performance Analysis**: Regularly review performance data and compare it against your KPIs. Identify trends and insights that can help optimize the campaign and enhance its effectiveness.

7. Troubleshoot and Address Issues

- **Problem-Solving**: Address any issues that arise promptly, such as technical glitches, content errors, or negative feedback. Have contingency plans in place to manage potential disruptions.

- **Support**: Provide support to your team and audience as needed. Ensure that any issues are resolved quickly to minimize impact on the campaign's success.

8. Document and Evaluate

- **Documentation**: Keep detailed records of the campaign's execution, including timelines, decisions made, and performance data. This documentation will be valuable for future campaigns.

- **Evaluation**: Conduct a thorough evaluation of the campaign's overall success. Assess what worked well and what could be improved. Gather feedback from team members and stakeholders to refine your approach.

By following these steps, you can ensure a smooth and effective launch of your marketing campaign across all selected channels. Proper execution is crucial to maximizing your campaign's reach and impact, setting the stage for achieving your marketing objectives and driving meaningful results.

COORDINATING TEAMS AND TOOLS: ENSURING ALIGNMENT BETWEEN MARKETING, SALES, AND OTHER DEPARTMENTS

1. Establish Clear Objectives and Goals

- **Unified Vision**: Ensure that all departments understand and share the campaign's objectives and goals. Align everyone's efforts towards common outcomes to prevent misalignment and confusion.

- **Goals Communication**: Clearly communicate the campaign's goals and expected results to all team members. Use written documents, presentations, and meetings to ensure comprehensive understanding.

2. Define Roles and Responsibilities

- **Role Clarity**: Clearly define the roles and responsibilities of each team involved in the campaign. Specify who is accountable for what tasks, such as content creation, campaign management, and customer engagement.

- **Responsibility Matrix**: Develop a responsibility matrix to map out who is responsible, accountable, consulted, and informed (RACI) for each aspect of the campaign. This helps in managing expectations and responsibilities.

3. Facilitate Cross-Departmental Communication

- **Regular Meetings**: Schedule regular meetings to facilitate communication between marketing, sales, and other departments. Use these meetings to discuss progress, address issues, and share updates.

- **Collaborative Tools**: Utilize collaborative tools and platforms, such as Slack, Microsoft Teams, or Asana, to enhance communication and ensure that all team members are up-to-date on campaign developments.

4. Integrate Technology and Tools

- **Unified Platforms**: Ensure that marketing, sales, and other departments use integrated tools and platforms for managing campaigns, tracking performance, and analyzing data. This helps maintain consistency and accuracy in reporting.

- **CRM Systems**: Use Customer Relationship Management (CRM) systems to track and manage customer interactions across departments. Ensure that marketing and sales teams have access to relevant customer data to tailor their approaches.

5. Align Marketing and Sales Efforts

- **Shared Insights**: Share insights and data between marketing and sales teams to ensure alignment in messaging and customer engagement strategies. Use data from marketing campaigns to inform sales strategies and vice versa.

- **Lead Management**: Implement processes for managing leads and tracking their progress from marketing to sales. Ensure that leads are properly qualified, nurtured, and handed off to sales teams in a timely manner.

6. Develop a Coordinated Content Strategy

- **Content Sharing**: Share content plans and assets between marketing and sales teams to ensure consistency in messaging and branding. Align content with sales materials and promotional strategies.

- **Feedback Loop**: Establish a feedback loop between departments to continuously improve content and messaging. Sales teams can provide valuable insights on customer reactions and needs.

7. Monitor and Adjust Collaborative Efforts

- **Performance Tracking**: Monitor the performance of collaborative efforts across departments. Track key metrics such as lead conversion rates, campaign engagement, and sales outcomes to assess effectiveness.

- **Adjust Strategies**: Be prepared to adjust strategies based on performance data and feedback from different teams. Foster an environment of continuous improvement and adaptability.

8. Address Conflicts and Issues Promptly

- **Conflict Resolution**: Address any conflicts or issues between departments quickly and effectively. Use a structured approach to resolve disputes and ensure that all teams remain focused on common goals.

- **Open Communication**: Encourage open and honest communication to prevent misunderstandings and ensure that all concerns are addressed. Foster a collaborative culture that values input from all departments.

9. Evaluate and Document Collaborative Efforts

- **Post-Campaign Review**: Conduct a post-campaign review to evaluate the effectiveness of cross-departmental coordination. Assess what worked well and identify areas for improvement.

- **Documentation**: Document lessons learned and best practices for future campaigns. Share these insights with all relevant teams to enhance future collaboration and campaign execution.

By effectively coordinating teams and tools, you can ensure that marketing, sales, and other departments work together seamlessly towards achieving campaign goals. Clear communication, integrated technology, and well-defined roles are key to maintaining alignment and driving successful outcomes.

REAL-TIME ADJUSTMENTS: MONITORING PERFORMANCE AND MAKING NECESSARY ADJUSTMENTS DURING THE CAMPAIGN

1. Set Up Real-Time Monitoring Tools

- **Analytics Platforms**: Use advanced analytics platforms such as Google Analytics, social media insights, and marketing dashboards to monitor campaign performance in real-time. Ensure that these tools are configured to track key metrics and provide immediate feedback.

- **Alerts and Notifications**: Set up alerts and notifications for significant changes in performance metrics, such as sudden drops in engagement or spikes in traffic. This helps you stay informed and responsive to potential issues.

2. Track Key Performance Indicators (KPIs)

- **Define KPIs**: Identify the key performance indicators (KPIs) relevant to your campaign objectives, such as conversion rates, click-through rates, engagement levels, and return on investment (ROI).

- **Monitor KPIs**: Continuously track these KPIs throughout the campaign to assess its effectiveness. Regularly review performance data to determine if the campaign is meeting its goals and where adjustments may be needed.

3. Analyze Performance Data

- **Data Interpretation**: Analyze performance data to understand trends and identify patterns. Look for insights that can inform adjustments, such as high-performing content or underperforming channels.

- **Segmentation**: Break down performance data by different segments, such as audience demographics or geographical locations, to gain a deeper understanding of what is working and what is not.

4. Make Data-Driven Adjustments

- **Content Optimization**: If certain content is underperforming, make adjustments such as revising the copy, changing visuals, or testing alternative messages. Use A/B testing to compare different versions and determine what resonates best with your audience.

- **Channel Adjustments**: Reallocate resources or shift focus between channels based on their performance. For example, if social media is outperforming email marketing, consider increasing your investment in social media ads.

- **Budget Reallocation**: Adjust your budget allocation based on real-time performance data. Increase spending on high-performing areas and reduce or eliminate spending on underperforming aspects of the campaign.

5. Respond to External Factors

- **Market Changes**: Be aware of external factors that may impact your campaign, such as market trends, competitor activities, or economic conditions. Adjust your strategy as needed to respond to these changes.

- **Customer Feedback**: Monitor customer feedback and engagement, including comments, reviews, and direct messages. Address any concerns or issues raised by your audience and make adjustments to improve their experience.

6. Maintain Flexibility and Adaptability

- **Quick Decisions**: Be prepared to make quick decisions based on real-time data and insights. Flexibility is crucial for addressing unforeseen challenges and capitalizing on emerging opportunities.

- **Continuous Improvement**: Embrace a mindset of continuous improvement. Regularly review campaign performance and make incremental adjustments to enhance effectiveness and achieve better results.

7. Communicate Adjustments to the Team

- **Update Team Members**: Keep all relevant team members informed about any adjustments made to the campaign. Ensure that everyone understands the reasons for the changes and how they impact their responsibilities.

- **Coordination**: Coordinate with other departments, such as sales and customer support, to ensure that any changes to the campaign are effectively communicated and implemented across all touchpoints.

8. Document Changes and Outcomes

- **Record Adjustments**: Document any changes made to the campaign and their impact on performance. This includes noting what adjustments were made, why they were necessary, and the resulting outcomes.

- **Post-Campaign Analysis**: After the campaign concludes, conduct a thorough analysis of the adjustments made and their effectiveness. Use these insights to inform future campaigns and improve your overall strategy.

Real-time adjustments are essential for maintaining the effectiveness of your marketing campaign and ensuring that it continues to meet its objectives. By monitoring performance closely, making data-driven decisions, and remaining adaptable, you can optimize your campaign in real-time and achieve better results.

CHAPTER 6: LEVERAGING DIGITAL MARKETING TOOLS

In today's fast-paced digital landscape, the right tools can make all the difference in executing a successful marketing campaign. Chapter 6 delves into the critical role of digital marketing tools and how they can be leveraged to enhance efficiency, optimize performance, and drive impactful results.

Digital marketing tools offer a wide range of functionalities, from automating repetitive tasks to providing deep insights into customer behavior and campaign effectiveness. This chapter will guide you through the essential tools and platforms that can elevate your marketing strategy, including analytics software, content management systems, and marketing automation platforms.

We will explore how to select the right tools for your specific needs, integrate them into your marketing stack, and use them to streamline processes, analyze performance, and foster better engagement with your audience. Additionally, we will discuss best practices for maximizing the potential of these tools and ensuring they contribute to your overall campaign success.

By the end of this chapter, you will have a comprehensive understanding of how to effectively utilize digital marketing tools to enhance your campaigns, improve operational efficiency, and achieve your marketing goals with greater precision and impact.

SEO AND SEM: OPTIMIZING CONTENT FOR SEARCH ENGINES AND MANAGING PAY-PER-CLICK CAMPAIGNS

1. Understanding SEO and SEM

- **SEO (Search Engine Optimization)**: SEO focuses on optimizing your website and content to improve organic search engine rankings. The goal is to increase visibility and attract more traffic through unpaid search results.

- **SEM (Search Engine Marketing)**: SEM involves managing paid search campaigns, such as Google Ads, to drive targeted traffic to your website. It includes pay-per-click (PPC) advertising and other paid search strategies to complement SEO efforts.

2. Optimizing Content for Search Engines

- **Keyword Research**: Conduct thorough keyword research to identify the terms and phrases your target audience uses to search for relevant products or services. Use tools like Google Keyword Planner, SEMrush, or Ahrefs to find high-value keywords.

  - **Long-Tail Keywords**: Focus on long-tail keywords that are more specific and less competitive. These can attract highly qualified traffic and improve conversion rates.

  - **Search Intent**: Consider the search intent behind keywords—whether users are looking for information, solutions, or making a purchase. Tailor your content to address these intents.

- **On-Page SEO**: Optimize individual pages on your website to enhance their search engine rankings.

- **Title Tags and Meta Descriptions**: Craft compelling and keyword-rich title tags and meta descriptions for each page. Ensure they accurately reflect the content and encourage clicks.

- **Headers and Subheaders**: Use header tags (H1, H2, H3, etc.) to structure your content and make it easier for both users and search engines to understand.

- **Content Quality**: Create high-quality, relevant, and engaging content that provides value to your audience. Address their questions and offer solutions to their problems.

- **Internal Linking**: Implement a strategic internal linking structure to help users navigate your site and distribute link equity across pages.

- **Image Optimization**: Optimize images by using descriptive filenames and alt text. Ensure images are compressed for fast loading times.

- **Technical SEO**: Address technical aspects of your website to improve its crawlability and indexing by search engines.

  - **Site Speed**: Optimize your website's loading speed by minimizing code, compressing images, and using caching.

  - **Mobile-Friendliness**: Ensure your site is mobile-responsive and provides a seamless experience across all devices.

  - **XML Sitemap**: Create and submit an XML sitemap to search engines to help them discover and index your pages.

o   **Robots.txt**: Use the robots.txt file to guide search engine crawlers on which pages to index and which to exclude.

- **Off-Page SEO**: Build authority and trustworthiness through external factors.

    o   **Backlinks**: Acquire high-quality backlinks from reputable sites to improve your site's authority and search engine rankings.

    o   **Social Signals**: Leverage social media to drive traffic and engagement, which can indirectly impact SEO.

3. Managing Pay-Per-Click Campaigns

- **Campaign Setup**: Create and configure PPC campaigns using platforms like Google Ads. Define your target audience, set budget limits, and select appropriate keywords.

    o   **Ad Groups**: Organize your campaigns into ad groups based on related keywords and themes. This improves ad relevance and quality scores.

    o   **Ad Copy**: Write compelling ad copy that includes relevant keywords, clear calls to action, and value propositions. Test different variations to determine what resonates best with your audience.

- **Bid Management**: Set and adjust bids for keywords to optimize ad placements and control costs. Use automated bidding strategies or manual adjustments based on performance data.

- Bid Strategies: Choose bid strategies such as manual CPC, enhanced CPC, or target CPA to align with your campaign goals.

- **Performance Tracking**: Monitor key metrics such as click-through rates (CTR), conversion rates, cost per click (CPC), and return on ad spend (ROAS). Use these metrics to evaluate the effectiveness of your PPC campaigns.

  - **Analytics Tools**: Utilize tools like Google Analytics and Google Ads reports to track and analyze campaign performance.

- **Optimization**: Continuously optimize your PPC campaigns based on performance data.

  - **Keyword Refinement**: Regularly review and update your keyword list to include new opportunities and exclude underperforming terms.

  - **Ad Testing**: Conduct A/B tests on ad copy, landing pages, and targeting options to improve campaign effectiveness.

  - **Budget Allocation**: Adjust your budget allocation based on performance, focusing on high-performing keywords and ads.

- **Remarketing**: Implement remarketing strategies to re-engage users who have previously interacted with your site but did not convert. Use tailored ads to encourage return visits and conversions.

4. Integrating SEO and SEM

- **Synergistic Strategy**: Combine SEO and SEM efforts to maximize visibility and traffic. Use insights from

PPC campaigns to inform SEO strategies and vice versa.

- o **Keyword Insights**: Analyze keyword performance data from both SEO and SEM to refine your overall keyword strategy.

- o **Content Opportunities**: Identify content opportunities and gaps based on data from both organic and paid search.

By effectively optimizing your content for search engines and managing pay-per-click campaigns, you can enhance your online visibility, drive targeted traffic, and achieve your marketing goals. Leveraging both SEO and SEM ensures a comprehensive approach to search marketing, maximizing your reach and impact.

SOCIAL MEDIA MARKETING: STRATEGIES FOR FACEBOOK, INSTAGRAM, LINKEDIN, TWITTER, AND EMERGING PLATFORMS

1. Facebook Marketing Strategies

- **Audience Targeting**: Utilize Facebook's advanced targeting options to reach specific demographics, interests, and behaviors. Create custom audiences based on past interactions, and use lookalike audiences to find new potential customers similar to your existing ones.

- **Content Variety**: Post a mix of content types, including text updates, images, videos, and live streams. Engage your audience with polls, questions, and interactive posts to drive participation.

- **Facebook Ads**: Use Facebook Ads Manager to create and manage ad campaigns. Implement strategies like A/B testing to optimize ad performance and adjust targeting based on real-time data.

- **Community Building**: Foster a sense of community by creating and engaging with Facebook Groups related to your industry. Share valuable content, answer questions, and participate in discussions to build relationships with your audience.

2. Instagram Marketing Strategies

- **Visual Appeal**: Focus on high-quality, visually appealing content that aligns with your brand's aesthetics. Use consistent colors, themes, and styles to create a cohesive brand presence.

- **Stories and Reels**: Leverage Instagram Stories and Reels to engage users with short, dynamic content. Use features like stickers, polls, and questions to interact with your audience in real-time.

- **Hashtags**: Research and use relevant hashtags to increase the visibility of your posts. Create branded hashtags to encourage user-generated content and build a community around your brand.

- **Influencer Collaborations**: Partner with influencers who align with your brand values and target audience. Collaborations can enhance credibility, reach, and engagement.

3. LinkedIn Marketing Strategies

- **Professional Content**: Share industry insights, company updates, and thought leadership content. Focus on content that adds value to professionals in your industry and demonstrates your expertise.

- **Networking and Engagement**: Connect with industry peers, join relevant groups, and participate in discussions to expand your professional network. Engage with other users' content by liking, commenting, and sharing.

- **LinkedIn Ads**: Use LinkedIn's ad options, including Sponsored Content, InMail, and Text Ads, to target professionals based on job title, industry, and company size. Tailor your ads to address the specific needs and interests of your audience.

- **Company Page Optimization**: Optimize your LinkedIn company page with a clear description, logo, and cover image. Regularly update your page with relevant content and job postings to attract potential employees and clients.

4. X Marketing Strategies

- **Timely Updates**: Use X for real-time updates, news, and conversations related to your industry. Share relevant content and participate in trending topics to increase visibility.

- **Engagement**: Engage with your audience by responding to tweets, retweeting user-generated content, and participating in X Chats. Use mentions and hashtags to join conversations and increase engagement.

- **X Ads**: Implement X Ads to promote tweets, accounts, or trends. Use targeting options to reach specific demographics and interests, and optimize campaigns based on performance data.

- **Visuals and Media**: Enhance tweets with images, GIFs, and videos to capture attention and increase engagement. Ensure media content is relevant and aligns with your brand's messaging.

5. Emerging Platforms

- **TikTok**: Embrace TikTok's creative and viral nature by creating short, engaging videos that align with trending challenges and themes. Use popular music and effects to enhance content appeal.

- **Snapchat**: Utilize Snapchat's ephemeral content and interactive features to engage younger audiences. Create Stories, filters, and geofilters to drive brand awareness and engagement.

- **Threads**: Engage with users on Threads, a text-based platform similar to X/Twitter, by sharing updates, joining discussions, and connecting with influencers. Tailor content to fit the platform's conversational style.

6. Best Practices Across Platforms

- **Consistency**: Maintain a consistent brand voice, message, and visual style across all social media platforms. This helps build brand recognition and trust.

- **Analytics and Monitoring**: Regularly review analytics and performance metrics to understand what content works best and refine your strategies accordingly. Monitor audience feedback and adjust your approach based on insights.

- **Adaptability**: Stay updated with platform changes and emerging trends. Be willing to adapt your strategies and content to align with new features and audience preferences.

By implementing effective strategies for each social media platform and staying adaptable to new trends, you can enhance your brand's online presence, engage with your audience, and achieve your marketing goals.

EMAIL MARKETING: BUILDING AND NURTURING EMAIL LISTS, CREATING EFFECTIVE EMAIL CAMPAIGNS

1. Building and Growing Your Email List

- **Lead Magnets**: Use lead magnets such as eBooks, whitepapers, webinars, or exclusive discounts to incentivize users to subscribe to your email list. Ensure that your lead magnets are relevant and valuable to your target audience.

- **Signup Forms**: Place email signup forms prominently on your website, including on landing pages, blog posts, and pop-ups. Keep forms simple, asking only for essential information like name and email address to maximize conversions.

- **Landing Pages**: Create dedicated landing pages for email signups, focusing on a compelling offer and a clear call to action. Test different versions to determine which designs and messaging drive the highest sign-up rates.

- **Social Media Integration**: Promote your email list on social media platforms. Share the benefits of subscribing and provide easy access to signup forms or landing pages.

- **Referral Programs**: Implement referral programs that encourage existing subscribers to refer friends or colleagues. Offer incentives for successful referrals to increase your list's reach.

2. Nurturing Your Email List

- **Welcome Series**: Design a welcome series for new subscribers to introduce them to your brand and provide valuable content. Include a thank-you email, an overview of what they can expect, and an initial offer or resource.

- **Segmentation**: Segment your email list based on criteria such as demographics, purchase history, or engagement levels. Tailor your messages to different segments to increase relevance and engagement.

- **Personalization**: Personalize your emails by addressing recipients by their first name and customizing content based on their preferences or behaviors. Use data to deliver targeted offers and recommendations.

- **Regular Engagement**: Maintain regular communication with your subscribers by sending consistent, valuable content. This keeps your brand top of mind and encourages ongoing engagement.

- **Re-Engagement Campaigns**: Identify inactive subscribers and create re-engagement campaigns to win them back. Offer special incentives or ask for feedback to understand why they became inactive.

3. Creating Effective Email Campaigns

- **Campaign Objectives**: Define clear objectives for each email campaign, such as driving traffic, increasing sales, or promoting an event. Align your content and call to action with these objectives.

- **Subject Lines**: Craft compelling and relevant subject lines to grab attention and encourage opens. Test different subject lines to determine what resonates best with your audience.

- **Email Content**: Create engaging content that delivers value to your subscribers. Include a mix of text, images, and calls to action that guide recipients towards the desired action.

- o **Visuals**: Use high-quality images and a clean design to make your emails visually appealing. Ensure that visuals are optimized for different devices and email clients.

- o **Copywriting**: Write clear, concise, and persuasive copy that aligns with your campaign objectives. Focus on benefits and use a conversational tone to connect with your audience.

- o **Calls to Action**: Include clear and actionable calls to action that guide recipients on what to do next. Use buttons or links to make it easy for them to take action.

- **A/B Testing**: Conduct A/B tests on various elements of your emails, such as subject lines, content, images, and calls to action. Analyze the results to determine what performs best and optimize future campaigns accordingly.

- **Responsive Design**: Ensure your emails are designed to be mobile-responsive. Test your emails on different devices and email clients to ensure they look good and function properly across all platforms.

- **Compliance**: Adhere to email marketing regulations such as GDPR, CAN-SPAM, and CCPA. Include clear opt-in and opt-out options in your emails and ensure that you are respecting subscriber preferences and privacy.

4. Analyzing and Optimizing Email Performance

- **Key Metrics**: Track key metrics such as open rates, click-through rates, conversion rates, and unsubscribe rates to gauge the effectiveness of your campaigns. Use these insights to refine your strategies and improve performance.

- **Feedback and Surveys**: Collect feedback from your subscribers through surveys or direct responses. Use this information to understand their needs and preferences, and adjust your email content and strategies accordingly.

- **Continuous Improvement**: Regularly review your email marketing performance and make data-driven adjustments. Experiment with new approaches, refine your segmentation and personalization, and stay updated with best practices.

By building and nurturing your email list effectively and creating compelling email campaigns, you can drive engagement, foster customer loyalty, and achieve your marketing objectives. Email marketing remains a powerful tool for connecting with your audience and delivering personalized, impactful messages.

CHAPTER 7: MEASURING AND ANALYZING PERFORMANCE

In the realm of marketing, understanding the impact of your efforts is crucial for ongoing success. Chapter 7 delves into the essential practices of measuring and analyzing performance to ensure your campaigns are not just executed but effectively optimized for maximum results.

Performance measurement is the cornerstone of effective marketing. It involves systematically tracking and evaluating various metrics to gauge how well your campaigns are meeting their objectives. This chapter will guide you through the key performance indicators (KPIs) and analytics tools necessary to gain actionable insights into your marketing activities.

We will explore methods for collecting and interpreting data, from website analytics to social media metrics, and how to use these insights to make informed decisions. Additionally, we'll discuss techniques for assessing the ROI of your campaigns, understanding customer behavior, and identifying areas for improvement.

By the end of this chapter, you will have a comprehensive understanding of how to measure and analyze your marketing performance, enabling you to refine your strategies, maximize your impact, and achieve your business goals with greater precision.

TRACKING METRICS: IDENTIFYING KEY PERFORMANCE INDICATORS (KPIS) FOR DIFFERENT TYPES OF CAMPAIGNS

1. Understanding Key Performance Indicators (KPIs)

Key Performance Indicators (KPIs) are measurable values that help you assess the effectiveness and success of your marketing campaigns. By tracking KPIs, you can evaluate how well your campaigns are performing against your goals and make data-driven decisions to enhance your strategies.

2. KPIs for Digital Marketing Campaigns

- **Website Traffic**: Monitor overall traffic to your website to gauge the effectiveness of digital campaigns in driving visitors.

    - **Sessions**: Total number of visits to your site, including repeated visits.

    - **Unique Visitors**: Number of individual users visiting your site, providing insights into reach and audience growth.

    - **Page Views**: Total number of pages viewed, indicating content engagement.

- **Conversion Rate**: Measure the percentage of visitors who take a desired action, such as completing a purchase or filling out a form.

    - **Form Submissions**: Number of completed contact or lead generation forms.

    - **E-Commerce Transactions**: Number of completed sales or purchases on your site.

- **Cost Per Acquisition (CPA)**: Calculate the average cost to acquire a new customer or lead through your campaigns.

  - o **Ad Spend vs. Conversions**: Compare total advertising expenditure to the number of conversions achieved.

- **Click-Through Rate (CTR)**: Assess the percentage of users who click on your ads or links compared to the number of times they are shown.

  - o **Ad Impressions vs. Clicks**: Track how often your ads are displayed and how frequently users interact with them.

- **Return on Investment (ROI)**: Evaluate the profitability of your campaigns by comparing the revenue generated to the cost of the campaign.

  - o **Revenue vs. Ad Spend**: Measure the total revenue generated from the campaign against the total amount spent.

3. KPIs for Social Media Campaigns

- **Engagement Rate**: Measure the level of interaction your content receives from your audience.

  - o **Likes, Shares, and Comments**: Track the number of likes, shares, and comments on your posts to gauge engagement.

  - o **Engagement Ratio**: Calculate the ratio of engagement interactions to the total number of followers or impressions.

- **Follower Growth**: Monitor changes in your social media follower count to assess the effectiveness of your social media strategies.

  - ○ **New Followers**: Track the number of new followers gained over a specific period.

- **Social Media Referral Traffic**: Measure the amount of traffic directed to your website from social media platforms.

  - ○ **Traffic Sources**: Analyze referral sources to determine which social platforms drive the most traffic.

- **Social Media Share of Voice**: Assess your brand's presence compared to competitors by tracking mentions and discussions.

  - ○ **Brand Mentions**: Count the number of times your brand is mentioned across social media.

4. KPIs for Email Marketing Campaigns

- **Open Rate**: Measure the percentage of recipients who open your emails.

  - ○ **Total Opens vs. Sent Emails**: Compare the total number of opens to the total number of emails sent.

- **Click-Through Rate (CTR)**: Track the percentage of recipients who click on links within your emails.

  - ○ **Clicks vs. Opens**: Assess how many users who opened the email engaged with the content.

- **Bounce Rate**: Monitor the percentage of emails that could not be delivered to recipients.

- o **Hard Bounces vs. Soft Bounces**: Differentiate between permanent delivery failures (hard bounces) and temporary issues (soft bounces).

- **Unsubscribe Rate**: Measure the percentage of recipients who opt out of your email list after receiving a campaign.

  - o **Unsubscribes vs. Sent Emails**: Track how many users unsubscribe relative to the total number of emails sent.

5. KPIs for Traditional Marketing Campaigns

- **Brand Awareness**: Evaluate the increase in brand recognition and recall resulting from traditional marketing efforts.

  - o **Survey Results**: Conduct surveys to measure brand awareness before and after the campaign.

- **Event Attendance**: Track the number of attendees at events or trade shows to gauge the success of promotional efforts.

  - o **RSVPs vs. Attendees**: Compare the number of RSVPs to actual attendance figures.

- **Direct Response**: Measure the direct responses to traditional marketing efforts, such as coupons or phone calls.

  - o **Coupon Redemptions**: Track the number of coupons redeemed as a result of a direct mail campaign.

By identifying and tracking these KPIs for various types of campaigns, you can gain valuable insights into the performance of your marketing activities. This data-driven approach allows you to make informed decisions, optimize your strategies, and achieve better results.

ANALYTICS TOOLS: USING GOOGLE ANALYTICS, SOCIAL MEDIA INSIGHTS, AND OTHER TOOLS TO GATHER DATA

1. Google Analytics

Google Analytics is a powerful tool for tracking and analyzing website performance, providing deep insights into user behavior, traffic sources, and campaign effectiveness. Here's how to leverage Google Analytics:

- **Traffic Analysis**: Monitor overall website traffic, including metrics such as sessions, users, page views, and bounce rate. Understand how different sources of traffic (organic search, paid search, referral, direct) contribute to your site's performance.

- **User Behavior**: Analyze user behavior on your site by tracking metrics like average session duration, pages per session, and exit pages. Identify which pages engage users and which ones cause them to leave.

- **Conversion Tracking**: Set up goals and events to track specific user actions, such as form submissions, product purchases, or content downloads. Measure conversion rates and identify areas where users drop off in the conversion funnel.

- **Audience Insights**: Gain insights into the demographics, interests, and geographic locations of your website visitors. Use this data to tailor your marketing strategies to better target and engage your audience.

- **Campaign Tracking**: Use UTM parameters to track the performance of specific marketing campaigns, such as email newsletters or paid ads. Analyze the effectiveness of different channels and campaigns in driving traffic and conversions.

2. Social Media Insights

Social media platforms provide built-in analytics tools to help you measure the performance of your social media efforts. Here's how to use these tools effectively:

- **Facebook Insights**: Track engagement metrics such as likes, comments, shares, and reach for your Facebook posts. Analyze your audience's demographics and behavior to refine your content strategy. Monitor page performance with metrics like page views, actions on the page, and follower growth.

- **Instagram Insights**: Measure the performance of your Instagram posts and stories, including metrics such as impressions, reach, engagement, and follower demographics. Use these insights to optimize your content and posting schedule.

- **Twitter Analytics**: Analyze tweet performance by tracking metrics such as impressions, engagements, and engagement rate. Review follower growth and demographic data to understand your audience better.

- **LinkedIn Analytics**: Evaluate the effectiveness of your LinkedIn posts and updates by monitoring metrics such as impressions, clicks, and engagement. Review the performance of your company page and track follower growth and demographics.

3. Email Marketing Analytics

Email marketing platforms offer analytics to track the performance of your email campaigns:

- **Open Rates**: Measure the percentage of recipients who open your emails. High open rates indicate effective subject lines and timing.

- **Click-Through Rates (CTR)**: Track the percentage of recipients who click on links within your emails. This metric helps assess the effectiveness of your content and calls to action.

- **Conversion Rates**: Analyze how many recipients complete the desired action, such as making a purchase or signing up for a webinar. This metric provides insights into the effectiveness of your email's content and offers.

- **Bounce Rates and Unsubscribes**: Monitor the percentage of emails that could not be delivered (bounces) and the number of unsubscribes. High bounce rates may indicate list quality issues, while high unsubscribe rates can signal content or targeting problems.

4. Other Analytics Tools

In addition to the major platforms mentioned, several other tools can provide valuable data insights:

- **Google Search Console**: Track your site's performance in Google search results, including impressions, clicks, and average position. Identify and address issues related to indexing, mobile usability, and search queries.

- **Hotjar**: Use Hotjar for heatmaps, session recordings, and user feedback to understand how visitors interact with your website. Analyze user behavior and identify areas for improvement.

- **SEMrush or Ahrefs**: Monitor your website's SEO performance, track keyword rankings, and analyze backlinks. Use these tools to identify SEO opportunities and evaluate your site's search engine visibility.

By effectively using these analytics tools, you can gather comprehensive data on your marketing performance. Analyzing this data enables you to make informed decisions, optimize your strategies, and achieve better results across your marketing channels.

REPORTING AND INSIGHTS: CREATING REPORTS THAT PROVIDE ACTIONABLE INSIGHTS FOR FUTURE CAMPAIGNS

1. Importance of Reporting

Effective reporting is crucial for understanding the outcomes of your marketing campaigns and for guiding future strategies. Reports translate raw data into actionable insights, helping you assess performance, identify strengths and weaknesses, and make informed decisions for upcoming campaigns.

2. Key Components of a Marketing Report

- **Executive Summary**: Provide a concise overview of the report's findings, including key metrics, major achievements, and areas needing improvement. This section should offer a quick snapshot of campaign performance for stakeholders who need a high-level understanding.

- **Campaign Objectives and Goals**: Restate the objectives and goals set for the campaign, and assess how well they were met. This context helps in evaluating the success of the campaign against the initial targets.

- **Performance Metrics**: Include detailed analysis of key performance indicators (KPIs) relevant to the campaign. Metrics should be presented in a clear format, often with visual aids such as charts and graphs, to illustrate trends and results.

  - **Traffic and Engagement**: Report on metrics like website traffic, page views, social media engagement, and email open rates.

- Conversions and Sales: Provide data on conversions, sales, lead generation, and other goal-specific metrics.

- Audience Insights: Analyze the demographics, interests, and behaviors of your target audience. Highlight any shifts in audience engagement or new insights gained during the campaign.

- ROI and Cost Analysis: Calculate the return on investment (ROI) by comparing the revenue generated to the campaign costs. Include a breakdown of expenditures to identify areas where budget allocation was effective or needs adjustment.

- Successes and Achievements: Highlight key successes, such as high-performing ads, successful content pieces, or particularly effective marketing channels. Provide examples and data to support these achievements.

- Challenges and Areas for Improvement: Identify any issues or challenges encountered during the campaign. Discuss factors that hindered performance and provide recommendations for addressing these issues in future campaigns.

3. Visualizing Data

Effective reporting often involves visualizing data to make complex information more understandable:

- Charts and Graphs: Use bar charts, line graphs, and pie charts to represent quantitative data. These visuals can help illustrate trends, comparisons, and proportions clearly.

- Tables and Dashboards: Incorporate tables and dashboards for detailed data presentation and real-time performance monitoring. Dashboards can provide a snapshot of multiple metrics in one view.

- **Heatmaps and Graphical Reports**: Use heatmaps and other graphical representations to visualize user interactions on your website or within your app.

4. Actionable Insights

Translate data into actionable insights by:

- **Identifying Trends**: Look for patterns in the data that indicate areas of success or concern. Use these trends to forecast future performance and guide strategic decisions.

- **Understanding Customer Behavior**: Analyze customer actions and preferences to refine your targeting and messaging. Tailor future campaigns based on these insights to better meet audience needs.

- **Testing and Optimization**: Apply learnings from the campaign to test new approaches and optimize future efforts. Use A/B testing results and performance data to experiment with different strategies.

5. Reporting Frequency and Distribution

- **Regular Updates**: Schedule regular reporting intervals (e.g., weekly, monthly, quarterly) to keep stakeholders informed and to track progress over time. Adjust the frequency based on campaign duration and stakeholder needs.

- **Stakeholder Communication**: Distribute reports to relevant stakeholders, including team members, executives, and clients. Ensure that reports are tailored to the audience's level of detail and focus.

6. Continuous Improvement

Use reports as a foundation for continuous improvement. Review findings, implement recommendations, and refine strategies based on insights gained. Establish a feedback loop to incorporate learnings into future campaigns, enhancing overall effectiveness.

By creating comprehensive and insightful reports, you equip yourself and your team with the knowledge needed to refine strategies, optimize performance, and drive successful marketing outcomes in future campaigns.

CHAPTER 8: OPTIMIZING AND SCALING CAMPAIGNS

As your marketing campaigns progress, the real challenge lies not just in executing them but in continuously optimizing and scaling for greater impact. Chapter 8 focuses on the essential strategies and techniques for refining your campaigns and expanding their reach to achieve even better results.

Optimization is an ongoing process that involves fine-tuning various elements of your campaign to enhance performance. From adjusting your messaging and creative assets to tweaking your targeting and budget allocations, this chapter will provide you with actionable insights to improve campaign effectiveness based on real-time data and feedback.

Scaling, on the other hand, involves expanding the successful aspects of your campaigns to reach a larger audience or increase their impact. This requires a strategic approach to replicating success across different channels, geographies, or audience segments while maintaining or improving ROI.

Throughout this chapter, you'll learn how to:

- **Analyze Performance Data**: Identify key performance drivers and areas for improvement based on detailed analytics.

- **Refine Campaign Elements**: Implement changes to your strategies, creatives, and targeting to boost performance.

- **Expand Successful Tactics**: Leverage proven strategies to scale your campaigns effectively and achieve broader reach.

- **Manage Resources Efficiently**: Allocate your budget and resources in a way that maximizes return while supporting growth.

By mastering these techniques, you'll be able to enhance your campaign performance, adapt to changing market conditions, and drive sustained growth.

A/B TESTING: CONDUCTING EXPERIMENTS TO DETERMINE THE MOST EFFECTIVE ELEMENTS OF YOUR CAMPAIGN

1. Introduction to A/B Testing

A/B testing, also known as split testing, is a method of comparing two versions of a marketing element to determine which performs better. This experimental approach allows you to make data-driven decisions by testing variations and measuring their impact on your campaign's performance. Whether you're optimizing email subject lines, ad copy, landing page designs, or call-to-action buttons, A/B testing provides valuable insights into what resonates best with your audience.

2. Setting Up Your A/B Test

- **Define Your Objective**: Clearly outline what you want to achieve with your A/B test. This could be increasing click-through rates, improving conversion rates, or enhancing engagement. Having a specific goal will guide your test design and help measure success.

- **Identify the Variable to Test**: Choose a single element to test at a time. This could be anything from the color of a call-to-action button to the headline of an ad. Testing one variable ensures that you can accurately determine which change led to the performance difference.

- **Create Variations**: Develop two or more versions of the element you're testing. For example, if you're testing email subject lines, create two different subject lines to compare. Ensure that each variation is distinct enough to potentially impact performance.

- **Determine Your Sample Size**: Establish how many participants or impressions you need for each variation to ensure statistically significant results. The sample size depends on your overall audience size and the expected impact of the changes.

3. Implementing the Test

- **Split Your Audience**: Randomly divide your audience into segments, ensuring each segment is exposed to only one variation. This prevents bias and ensures that the results are attributable to the changes you made, not external factors.

- **Run the Test**: Execute your A/B test by delivering the variations to the respective segments. Make sure that the test duration is long enough to gather sufficient data but not so long that external factors skew the results.

- **Monitor Performance**: Track the performance of each variation using your chosen KPIs. This might include metrics such as click-through rates, conversion rates, or engagement levels. Ensure that you monitor the test continuously to address any issues that might arise.

4. Analyzing Results

- **Compare Performance**: Analyze the data collected from each variation to determine which performed better against your defined objective. Use statistical methods to assess whether the differences in performance are statistically significant.

- **Interpret Insights**: Understand why one variation outperformed the other. Look for patterns or insights that can inform future decisions. For example, if a certain headline led to higher engagement, consider what elements of that headline might have contributed to its success.

- **Document Findings**: Record the results and insights from your A/B test. Documenting your findings helps build a knowledge base for future testing and decision-making. Include details about the test setup, results, and any conclusions drawn.

5. Implementing Changes

- **Apply Learnings**: Use the insights gained from your A/B test to make informed changes to your campaign. Implement the successful variation and consider testing additional elements to continue refining your approach.

- **Iterate and Repeat**: A/B testing is an ongoing process. Continuously test new hypotheses and refine your strategies based on the results. Each test builds on previous learnings, helping you optimize your campaigns for better performance over time.

6. Best Practices for A/B Testing

- **Test One Variable at a Time**: Focus on one element per test to accurately measure its impact.

- **Ensure Statistical Significance**: Use an adequate sample size and statistical methods to validate your results.

- **Consider External Factors**: Be aware of any external factors that might influence your test results, such as seasonality or market trends.

- **Document Everything**: Keep detailed records of your tests to track what works and what doesn't over time.

By systematically applying A/B testing, you can gain valuable insights into which elements of your campaigns are most effective. This approach allows you to make data-driven decisions, optimize performance, and achieve better results in your marketing efforts.

CONVERSION RATE OPTIMIZATION: TECHNIQUES FOR IMPROVING THE CONVERSION RATES OF YOUR MARKETING EFFORTS

1. Understanding Conversion Rate Optimization (CRO)

Conversion Rate Optimization (CRO) involves enhancing various aspects of your marketing efforts to increase the percentage of visitors who take a desired action, such as making a purchase, signing up for a newsletter, or filling out a contact form. Effective CRO is crucial for maximizing the return on your marketing investments by turning more of your audience into customers or leads.

2. Analyzing Current Performance

- **Measure Conversion Rates**: Begin by calculating your current conversion rates for different channels or campaigns. Use metrics like the percentage of visitors who complete a desired action out of the total number of visitors.

- **Identify Weak Points**: Analyze where visitors drop off in the conversion funnel. Use tools like Google Analytics, heatmaps, and session recordings to understand user behavior and pinpoint obstacles that hinder conversions.

3. Improving Website and Landing Page Design

- **Optimize Landing Pages**: Ensure that landing pages are designed to drive conversions. Key elements include a clear and compelling headline, engaging visuals, and a strong call-to-action (CTA). Keep the layout clean and focus on a single, specific goal.

- **Enhance User Experience (UX)**: Improve overall website usability by ensuring fast load times, mobile responsiveness, and intuitive navigation. A seamless user experience reduces frustration and keeps visitors engaged.

- **A/B Testing**: Continuously test different versions of your landing pages, CTAs, and other critical elements to determine which variations lead to higher conversion rates. Experiment with different headlines, button colors, and layouts to find the most effective combinations.

4. Crafting Compelling Calls-to-Action

- **Clear and Direct CTAs**: Ensure that your CTAs are easy to find and clearly communicate the action you want users to take. Use actionable language and create a sense of urgency when appropriate.

- **Visual Appeal**: Design CTAs that stand out visually. Use contrasting colors and prominent placement to draw attention. Test different designs and wording to see what resonates best with your audience.

5. Leveraging Social Proof

- **Customer Reviews and Testimonials**: Display positive reviews and testimonials prominently to build trust and credibility. Social proof can reassure potential customers and encourage them to take action.

- **Case Studies and Success Stories**: Share detailed case studies and success stories that highlight how your product or service has benefited other customers. This helps to illustrate the value and effectiveness of your offerings.

6. Personalization and Targeting

- **Tailor Content to Audience Segments**: Personalize your content based on user behavior, preferences, and demographics. Use dynamic content and targeted messaging to address the specific needs and interests of different audience segments.

- **Implement Retargeting**: Use retargeting strategies to reach visitors who have previously interacted with your site but did not convert. Tailor your ads and offers to remind and encourage them to return and complete the desired action.

7. Streamlining the Conversion Path

- **Simplify Forms**: Reduce the number of fields and steps in your forms to minimize friction and increase completion rates. Only ask for essential information and consider using progressive disclosure to collect additional details later.

- **Enhance Checkout Process**: For e-commerce sites, optimize the checkout process to minimize cart abandonment. Ensure that the process is straightforward, secure, and includes clear progress indicators.

8. Analyzing and Adjusting

- **Monitor Performance**: Continuously track conversion rates and user behavior to gauge the effectiveness of your optimization efforts. Use data to identify trends and areas for further improvement.

- **Iterate and Optimize**: Based on your analysis, make iterative changes to your campaigns and website elements. Regularly review and adjust your strategies to ensure ongoing improvements in conversion rates.

9. Tools and Resources

- **Conversion Rate Optimization Tools**: Utilize tools such as Google Optimize, Optimizely, and Unbounce to conduct A/B testing, create optimized landing pages, and analyze user behavior.

- **Heatmaps and Session Recordings**: Use tools like Hotjar or Crazy Egg to visualize where users click, scroll, and interact on your site. This helps to identify areas that may require improvement.

By implementing these techniques, you can enhance the effectiveness of your marketing efforts and achieve higher conversion rates. CRO is an ongoing process that involves continuously testing, analyzing, and refining your strategies to ensure that you are effectively turning visitors into customers and maximizing the impact of your marketing campaigns.

SCALING SUCCESSFUL CAMPAIGNS: EXPANDING REACH AND IMPACT WITHOUT LOSING EFFECTIVENESS

1. Introduction to Scaling

Scaling successful campaigns involves expanding their reach and impact to achieve greater results while maintaining or improving effectiveness. It's about taking proven strategies and replicating their success on a larger scale. This process requires careful planning, resource allocation, and continuous optimization to ensure that growth doesn't compromise the quality or performance of your campaigns.

2. Analyzing Success

- **Evaluate Performance Metrics**: Before scaling, assess the success of your initial campaigns. Review performance metrics, such as conversion rates, engagement levels, and ROI, to understand what elements contributed to their success.

- **Identify Key Drivers**: Determine the key factors that drove success in your campaign. This could include specific audience segments, channels, or messaging strategies that performed particularly well.

3. Developing a Scaling Strategy

- **Replicate Successful Tactics**: Identify the elements of your campaign that can be replicated across new channels or markets. For example, if a particular ad creative performed well, consider using it in other digital platforms or geographic regions.

- **Expand Audience Reach**: Use audience segmentation and targeting to reach new potential customers. Utilize lookalike audiences based on your most engaged or converting customers to find similar prospects.

- **Increase Budget Gradually**: Scale your budget in a controlled manner to avoid overspending. Gradually increase your investment based on the incremental success and performance data of your expanded efforts.

4. Optimizing for Larger Audiences

- **Maintain Quality and Relevance**: As you scale, ensure that your messaging remains relevant and personalized for the expanded audience. Adjust content and offers to fit the needs and preferences of new audience segments.

- **Monitor and Adjust**: Continuously track the performance of scaled campaigns. Be prepared to make adjustments based on real-time data to address any issues that arise as you reach a larger audience.

5. Leveraging New Channels

- **Explore Additional Platforms**: Identify and test new marketing channels where your audience is active. For example, if your initial campaign focused on social media, consider expanding to email marketing, content marketing, or other digital advertising platforms.

- **Adapt Strategies for Each Channel**: Tailor your strategies to fit the unique characteristics of each new channel. Customize your content, targeting, and budget allocation to align with the channel's audience and format.

6. Ensuring Operational Efficiency

- **Streamline Processes**: As you scale, ensure that your marketing processes and workflows are efficient.

Automate repetitive tasks, such as ad placements and performance tracking, to manage larger campaigns effectively.

- **Allocate Resources Wisely**: Distribute your resources, including team members and budget, to support scaled efforts. Ensure that you have the necessary tools and personnel to handle increased campaign activities.

7. Building on Insights

- **Use Data-Driven Insights**: Apply insights from scaled campaigns to refine your strategies further. Analyze performance data to identify trends, successful tactics, and areas for improvement.

- **Iterate and Innovate**: Continuously test new approaches and innovative strategies as you scale. Use learnings from previous campaigns to drive new ideas and improvements.

8. Managing Risks

- **Monitor for Diminished Returns**: Be aware of potential diminishing returns as you scale. Keep an eye on metrics to ensure that increased investment continues to deliver proportional gains in performance.

- **Address Market Saturation**: Avoid oversaturation by carefully managing the frequency and placement of your campaigns. Balance your outreach to maintain audience engagement and prevent ad fatigue.

9. Success Stories and Case Studies

- **Learn from Others**: Study case studies and success stories of similar campaigns that have successfully scaled. Learn from their strategies and apply relevant insights to your own scaling efforts.

- **Document Your Journey**: Keep detailed records of your scaling process, including strategies, challenges, and outcomes. Documenting your experiences helps build a knowledge base for future scaling initiatives.

Scaling successful campaigns requires a strategic approach to expand reach and impact while maintaining effectiveness. By analyzing success, optimizing for larger audiences, and managing resources efficiently, you can grow your campaigns and achieve greater results without sacrificing performance.

CHAPTER 9: CASE STUDIES AND REAL-WORLD EXAMPLES

In the world of marketing, theory is often best understood through practical application. Chapter 9 delves into case studies and real-world examples to illustrate how the strategies and techniques discussed in previous chapters come to life. By examining actual campaigns and their outcomes, you will gain a deeper understanding of how successful marketing initiatives are designed, executed, and optimized.

This chapter provides a detailed look at a range of case studies across different industries and campaign types. Each case study offers insights into the challenges faced, the strategies employed, and the results achieved. These real-world examples serve as valuable learning tools, highlighting best practices, common pitfalls, and innovative approaches that have driven success.

Key areas covered in this chapter include:

- **Detailed Case Studies**: In-depth analyses of specific campaigns that achieved notable success. Understand the context, objectives, and methodologies that led to their outcomes.

- **Lessons Learned**: Key takeaways from each case study, including what worked well and what could have been improved. Apply these lessons to enhance your own marketing efforts.

- **Industry Insights**: Examples from various sectors to showcase how different industries tackle similar challenges with unique strategies.

- **Innovative Approaches**: Highlighting creative and unconventional methods that have set certain campaigns apart from the competition.

By studying these examples, you will gain practical insights and actionable strategies to apply to your own marketing campaigns, helping you to refine your approach and drive better results.

SUCCESSFUL CAMPAIGNS: DETAILED ANALYSIS OF SUCCESSFUL MARKETING CAMPAIGNS FROM VARIOUS INDUSTRIES

Examining successful marketing campaigns provides valuable insights into effective strategies, innovative tactics, and industry-specific approaches. This section highlights notable campaigns across different sectors, offering a detailed analysis of what made them successful and how you can apply similar principles to your own marketing efforts.

1. Nike's "Just Do It" Campaign

Overview: Launched in 1988, Nike's "Just Do It" campaign is one of the most iconic marketing initiatives in history. The campaign's goal was to inspire and motivate athletes of all levels, connecting Nike's brand with the broader concept of determination and perseverance.

Strategy and Execution:

- **Brand Messaging**: The campaign's core message, "Just Do It," was simple, yet powerful. It resonated with a wide audience by promoting a universal message of self-belief and action.

- **Celebrity Endorsements**: Nike featured high-profile athletes like Michael Jordan and Serena Williams, adding credibility and appeal to the campaign.

- **Emotional Appeal**: The campaign's emotional resonance was amplified through motivational storytelling and visuals that emphasized personal achievement.

Results:

- **Brand Positioning**: Nike solidified its position as a leading sportswear brand, increasing its market share and brand recognition.

- **Revenue Growth**: The campaign contributed to a significant boost in sales, with Nike's revenue growing from $877 million in 1988 to over $9 billion in 1998.

Key Takeaway: Nike's campaign illustrates the power of a strong, simple message and emotional appeal combined with effective celebrity endorsements.

2. Old Spice's "The Man Your Man Could Smell Like"

Overview: In 2010, Old Spice launched the "The Man Your Man Could Smell Like" campaign, which aimed to rejuvenate its brand image and appeal to a younger audience. The campaign featured a humorous, over-the-top character played by actor Isaiah Mustafa.

Strategy and Execution:

- **Humor and Creativity**: The campaign used humor and absurdity to stand out, creating memorable and shareable content.

- **Interactive Engagement**: Old Spice engaged with the audience through a series of personalized video responses to tweets and comments, further enhancing the campaign's reach.

- **Social Media Savvy**: Leveraging platforms like YouTube and Twitter, the campaign went viral, generating millions of views and interactions.

Results:

- **Sales Increase**: Old Spice saw a 125% increase in sales of the featured products within a month of the campaign's launch.

- **Brand Perception**: The campaign successfully repositioned Old Spice as a modern, relevant brand, appealing to both men and women.

Key Takeaway: Old Spice's campaign demonstrates the effectiveness of humor and interactive engagement in creating viral content and revitalizing a brand.

3. Coca-Cola's "Share a Coke"

Overview: Coca-Cola's "Share a Coke" campaign, launched in 2011, replaced the brand's iconic logo on bottles with popular names and phrases, encouraging consumers to find and share their personalized Coke bottles.

Strategy and Execution:

- **Personalization**: By featuring individual names and messages, Coca-Cola created a personal connection with consumers.

- **Social Media Integration**: The campaign encouraged social sharing by asking people to post photos of their personalized bottles, boosting visibility and engagement.

- **Targeted Marketing**: Coca-Cola tailored the campaign to different markets, using region-specific names and phrases to enhance relevance.

Results:

- **Increased Sales**: Coca-Cola experienced a significant increase in sales, with some markets reporting up to a 4% rise in sales during the campaign period.

- **Enhanced Brand Engagement**: The campaign generated a substantial amount of user-generated content and social media interaction, strengthening brand loyalty and engagement.

Key Takeaway: Coca-Cola's campaign highlights the power of personalization and social media to drive consumer engagement and sales.

4. Apple's "Get a Mac"

Overview: The "Get a Mac" campaign, running from 2006 to 2009, featured a series of humorous ads comparing Mac and PC computers. The campaign aimed to highlight the advantages of Mac computers over PCs.

Strategy and Execution:

- **Comparative Advertising**: The campaign used a direct comparison between Mac and PC, highlighting Mac's benefits in a humorous and relatable manner.

- **Consistent Branding**: Apple maintained a consistent tone and style across all ads, reinforcing its brand identity.

- **Targeted Messaging**: The ads focused on key pain points for PC users, such as security issues and system crashes, positioning Macs as a more reliable choice.

Results:

- **Market Share Growth**: Apple saw a significant increase in market share for Mac computers during and after the campaign.

- **Increased Brand Awareness**: The campaign helped solidify Apple's reputation as an innovative and user-friendly brand.

Key Takeaway: Apple's campaign demonstrates the effectiveness of comparative advertising and consistent branding in highlighting product advantages and increasing market share.

5. Dove's "Real Beauty"

Overview: Dove's "Real Beauty" campaign, launched in 2004, aimed to challenge traditional beauty standards by featuring real women of diverse shapes, sizes, and ages in its advertising.

Strategy and Execution:

- **Inclusive Messaging**: The campaign promoted body positivity and inclusivity, resonating with a broad audience and aligning with Dove's brand values.

- **Emotional Impact**: Dove used powerful, authentic storytelling to connect with consumers on an emotional level.

- **Integrated Marketing**: The campaign extended beyond traditional advertising to include social media, public relations, and content marketing.

Results:

- **Positive Brand Image**: Dove's campaign significantly enhanced its brand image, positioning it as a champion of real beauty and inclusivity.

- **Increased Sales**: Dove experienced substantial growth in sales and market share as a result of the campaign's success.

Key Takeaway: Dove's campaign illustrates the impact of authentic, values-driven marketing in building a positive brand image and driving sales.

By analyzing these successful campaigns, you can gain insights into various strategies and techniques that contributed to their achievements. Applying similar approaches to your own marketing efforts can help you achieve greater success and drive meaningful results.

LESSONS LEARNED: KEY TAKEAWAYS AND LESSONS FROM BOTH SUCCESSFUL AND FAILED CAMPAIGNS

Analyzing both successful and failed campaigns provides valuable insights into what works and what doesn't in marketing. Understanding these lessons helps to refine strategies, avoid common pitfalls, and leverage best practices for future campaigns. Here are key takeaways and lessons drawn from a range of campaigns:

1. Importance of Clear Objectives

- **Success**: Successful campaigns like Nike's "Just Do It" illustrate the power of having clear, well-defined objectives. Nike's goal was to inspire and connect with athletes, which guided their messaging and execution.

- **Failure**: Campaigns that lack clear objectives often struggle to align messaging with goals. For example, some early digital marketing campaigns failed because they did not set specific targets or measure success effectively.

Lesson: Always establish clear objectives and align your campaign strategies to these goals. This helps ensure that every aspect of the campaign is focused and relevant.

2. The Power of Audience Understanding

- **Success**: Dove's "Real Beauty" campaign succeeded by deeply understanding and addressing its audience's desires for authenticity and inclusivity. This resonated strongly with consumers, leading to increased brand loyalty and sales.

- **Failure**: Campaigns that fail to understand their audience often miss the mark. For instance, some brands have faced backlash for campaigns that were perceived as out of touch or insensitive to their target audience's values.

Lesson: Invest in thorough audience research and segmentation. Tailor your messaging and content to address the specific needs, preferences, and values of your target audience.

3. The Role of Creativity and Innovation

- **Success**: Old Spice's "The Man Your Man Could Smell Like" campaign thrived on its innovative use of humor and interactive engagement. This creativity set it apart and drove viral success.

- **Failure**: Conversely, campaigns that lack creativity or rely on clichéd approaches often fail to capture attention. For example, generic ads with uninspired messaging may get lost in the noise of today's crowded marketing landscape.

Lesson: Embrace creativity and innovation in your campaigns. Stand out from the competition by offering unique, memorable experiences that capture and hold your audience's attention.

4. Effective Use of Data and Analytics

- **Success**: Coca-Cola's "Share a Coke" campaign leveraged data to personalize marketing efforts and optimize performance. By analyzing consumer data, Coca-Cola effectively targeted and engaged its audience.

- **Failure**: Campaigns that neglect data and analytics often face challenges in performance measurement and optimization. For example, some campaigns have failed due to a lack of insights into what resonates with the audience or where improvements are needed.

Lesson: Use data and analytics to inform your strategies. Monitor campaign performance regularly and adjust tactics based on real-time insights to enhance effectiveness.

5. The Significance of Consistency

- **Success**: Apple's "Get a Mac" campaign succeeded due to its consistent branding and messaging. The campaign maintained a uniform tone and style, reinforcing Apple's brand identity and values.

- **Failure**: Inconsistent branding can dilute a campaign's impact. Some campaigns have faltered because they lacked a cohesive message or varied too much in style and tone.

Lesson: Ensure consistency across all elements of your campaign, including messaging, visuals, and tone. Consistency helps build a strong, recognizable brand and reinforces your key messages.

6. The Impact of Timing and Context

- **Success**: Many successful campaigns, such as Nike's "Just Do It," were well-timed and aligned with broader cultural or societal trends, enhancing their relevance and impact.

- **Failure**: Timing issues can undermine a campaign's effectiveness. For instance, campaigns launched during economic downturns or sensitive times may be perceived as out of touch or inappropriate.

Lesson: Consider the timing and context of your campaign. Align your initiatives with current trends and events to maximize relevance and resonance.

7. The Importance of Testing and Iteration

- **Success**: Campaigns that incorporate A/B testing and iterative improvements, like Old Spice's interactive responses, often achieve better results by refining and optimizing their approach based on feedback.

- **Failure**: Campaigns that skip testing and iteration may miss opportunities for improvement. For example, some campaigns have underperformed due to a lack of pre-launch testing or failure to adjust based on early feedback.

Lesson: Continuously test and iterate your campaigns. Use A/B testing and other methods to refine your strategies and enhance performance over time.

8. The Role of Authenticity

- **Success**: Dove's "Real Beauty" campaign succeeded due to its authentic approach to beauty standards, creating a genuine connection with consumers and reinforcing brand values.

- **Failure**: Campaigns that come across as inauthentic or superficial often fail to engage audiences. For example, campaigns that attempt to mimic trends without a genuine connection to the brand may be perceived as disingenuous.

Lesson: Ensure that your campaigns are authentic and align with your brand's values and mission. Authenticity builds trust and fosters stronger connections with your audience.

By learning from both successful and failed campaigns, you can develop more effective marketing strategies and improve your chances of achieving your campaign goals. Implement these lessons to enhance your campaign planning, execution, and overall performance.

APPLYING INSIGHTS: HOW TO APPLY INSIGHTS FROM CASE STUDIES TO YOUR OWN CAMPAIGNS

Analyzing successful and failed campaigns provides valuable lessons, but the real challenge lies in translating these insights into actionable strategies for your own marketing efforts. Here's how to effectively apply the lessons learned from case studies to enhance your own campaigns:

1. Translate Objectives into Actionable Goals

Insight: Successful campaigns often begin with clear, well-defined objectives, as seen in Nike's "Just Do It" campaign.

Application:

- **Define Specific Goals**: Translate the broad objectives of successful campaigns into specific, actionable goals for your own campaigns. For instance, if a campaign's success was driven by increased brand engagement, set clear targets for engagement metrics such as likes, shares, and comments.

- **Align Strategies with Goals**: Ensure that every aspect of your campaign, from messaging to channel selection, is aligned with these goals to maintain focus and coherence.

2. Understand and Segment Your Audience

Insight: Effective campaigns, like Dove's "Real Beauty," deeply understand and segment their audience.

Application:

- **Conduct Audience Research**: Use insights from case studies to refine your audience research. Employ techniques like surveys, focus groups, and social listening to gain a nuanced understanding of your target audience.

- **Create Detailed Buyer Personas**: Develop detailed buyer personas based on insights from successful campaigns. Tailor your messaging and content to these personas to ensure relevance and resonance.

3. Embrace Creativity and Innovation

Insight: Creativity and innovation play a crucial role in campaign success, as demonstrated by Old Spice's humorous and interactive approach.

Application:

- **Foster Creative Thinking**: Encourage your team to think creatively and explore unconventional ideas. Look for unique angles or approaches that differentiate your campaign from competitors.

- **Experiment with Formats**: Experiment with various content formats and styles, such as videos, interactive elements, and humor, to find what resonates best with your audience.

4. Leverage Data for Decision Making

Insight: Successful campaigns like Coca-Cola's "Share a Coke" effectively use data to drive decisions.

Application:

- **Implement Data Analytics**: Utilize data analytics tools to gather insights into your campaign's performance. Track metrics such as engagement rates, conversion rates, and customer feedback to guide your decisions.

- **Adjust Based on Insights**: Regularly review data and adjust your strategies based on performance insights.

This iterative approach helps optimize your campaign in real-time.

5. Maintain Consistent Branding

Insight: Consistent branding, as seen in Apple's "Get a Mac" campaign, reinforces brand identity and messaging.

Application:

- **Develop a Brand Style Guide**: Create and adhere to a brand style guide that outlines your campaign's tone, visuals, and messaging. This ensures consistency across all campaign elements.

- **Align Across Channels**: Ensure that your messaging and branding are consistent across all marketing channels, from social media to email campaigns.

6. Consider Timing and Context

Insight: Timing and context significantly impact campaign effectiveness, as demonstrated by Coca-Cola's alignment with cultural trends.

Application:

- **Plan Campaign Timing**: Consider the timing of your campaign relative to industry events, seasonal trends, and current events. Align your campaign launch to maximize relevance and impact.

- **Monitor Contextual Factors**: Stay aware of external factors that might influence your campaign's reception. Be prepared to adjust your strategy in response to changes in context.

7. Test and Iterate

Insight: Testing and iteration, as seen in Old Spice's approach, enhance campaign effectiveness.

Application:

- **Conduct A/B Testing**: Implement A/B testing for different elements of your campaign, such as headlines, visuals, and calls to action. Use the results to refine and optimize your approach.

- **Gather Feedback**: Collect feedback from your audience and stakeholders to identify areas for improvement. Make iterative adjustments based on this feedback.

8. Ensure Authenticity

Insight: Authenticity, exemplified by Dove's campaign, builds trust and fosters strong connections with the audience.

Application:

- **Align with Brand Values**: Ensure that your campaign aligns with your brand's core values and mission. Authentic messaging should reflect your brand's genuine identity and commitment.

- **Be Transparent**: Communicate openly and honestly with your audience. Authenticity is reinforced through transparency and a genuine connection.

By applying these insights from successful and failed campaigns, you can enhance your own marketing strategies and drive better results. Use these lessons to guide your planning, execution, and optimization processes, ensuring that your campaigns are both effective and impactful.

CHAPTER 10: FUTURE TRENDS AND INNOVATIONS

As the marketing landscape continuously evolves, staying ahead of emerging trends and innovations is crucial for maintaining a competitive edge. Chapter 10 delves into the future of marketing, exploring the trends and technologies that are set to shape the industry in the coming years. This chapter aims to provide a forward-looking perspective on how these advancements will impact marketing strategies, consumer behavior, and the overall effectiveness of campaigns.

In this chapter, we will examine the cutting-edge developments in digital marketing, including advancements in artificial intelligence, data analytics, and immersive technologies such as virtual and augmented reality. We will also explore the rise of new marketing channels and platforms, as well as shifts in consumer expectations and behavior driven by technological innovation.

By understanding and adapting to these future trends, marketers can better prepare for the challenges and opportunities that lie ahead. Whether you're looking to leverage the latest technology to enhance your campaigns or anticipate changes in consumer preferences, this chapter will equip you with the knowledge to stay ahead in an ever-evolving field.

EMERGING TECHNOLOGIES: IMPACT OF AI, VR, AR, AND OTHER TECHNOLOGIES ON MARKETING CAMPAIGNS

As technology continues to advance at a rapid pace, new innovations are revolutionizing the marketing landscape. Emerging technologies such as artificial intelligence (AI), virtual reality (VR), augmented reality (AR), and other cutting-edge tools are reshaping how marketers approach campaigns and engage with their audiences. Here's a closer look at how these technologies are impacting marketing efforts:

1. Artificial Intelligence (AI)

Overview: AI is transforming marketing by automating processes, analyzing vast amounts of data, and providing personalized experiences. AI-powered tools and algorithms enable marketers to optimize their strategies more efficiently and effectively.

Impact on Marketing Campaigns:

- **Personalization**: AI enables advanced personalization by analyzing consumer behavior, preferences, and interactions. This allows marketers to deliver highly targeted content, recommendations, and advertisements tailored to individual users. For example, Netflix uses AI to suggest shows and movies based on viewing history.

- **Chatbots and Customer Service**: AI-driven chatbots provide instant customer support, handling inquiries and resolving issues 24/7. This enhances user experience and frees up human resources for more complex tasks. Companies like Sephora use AI chatbots to offer personalized beauty advice and product recommendations.

- **Predictive Analytics**: AI helps predict future trends and consumer behavior by analyzing historical data. This allows marketers to make data-driven decisions and forecast campaign performance. For instance, Amazon utilizes predictive analytics to optimize inventory and marketing strategies based on anticipated demand.

2. Virtual Reality (VR)

Overview: VR creates immersive, computer-generated environments that users can interact with in a simulated space. This technology offers a unique way to engage audiences by providing them with virtual experiences.

Impact on Marketing Campaigns:

- **Enhanced Brand Experiences**: VR allows brands to create immersive experiences that engage consumers in a novel way. For example, IKEA's VR kitchen experience lets customers explore and interact with different kitchen designs before making a purchase.

- **Product Demonstrations**: VR enables detailed product demonstrations and simulations, helping customers visualize how products work or how they would look in their own environment. For example, real estate companies use VR to offer virtual property tours.

- **Event Marketing**: Brands can host virtual events and experiences, expanding their reach and engaging a global audience. The use of VR in events like product launches or trade shows can create memorable experiences that drive brand awareness.

3. Augmented Reality (AR)

Overview: AR overlays digital information onto the real world through devices like smartphones or AR glasses. It enhances users' interactions with their physical surroundings by integrating virtual elements.

Impact on Marketing Campaigns:

- **Interactive Advertising**: AR enables interactive ad experiences that blend the digital and physical worlds. For instance, Pepsi's AR-enabled vending machines allowed users to interact with virtual elements, creating a fun and engaging experience.

- **Virtual Try-Ons**: AR technology is used for virtual try-ons in retail, allowing customers to see how products like clothing, accessories, or makeup would look on them without physically trying them on. Brands like L'Oréal and Warby Parker utilize AR for virtual try-on solutions.

- **Enhanced Engagement**: AR can create engaging scavenger hunts or location-based experiences that encourage user participation and interaction. For example, Pokémon GO utilized AR to blend gaming with real-world exploration, driving massive user engagement.

4. Other Emerging Technologies

Overview: Several other technologies are also influencing marketing strategies, including blockchain for transparency, the Internet of Things (IoT) for connected devices, and 5G for faster and more reliable connectivity.

Impact on Marketing Campaigns:

- **Blockchain**: Provides transparency and security in transactions, allowing marketers to build trust with consumers by ensuring data integrity and reducing fraud. Brands are exploring blockchain for secure advertising and verifying the authenticity of digital content.

- **IoT**: Connects everyday devices to the internet, enabling new marketing opportunities through data collection and personalized interactions. For example, smart home devices can offer targeted promotions based on user behavior and preferences.

- **5G**: Enhances connectivity and speeds up data transfer, enabling more seamless experiences for mobile users. 5G supports high-quality video streaming, real-time interactions, and advanced applications that rely on fast and reliable internet access.

By leveraging these emerging technologies, marketers can create more innovative, engaging, and personalized campaigns that stand out in a competitive landscape. Embracing these advancements will not only enhance the effectiveness of your marketing strategies but also position your brand as a leader in adopting the latest trends and technologies.

CHANGING CONSUMER BEHAVIOR: ADAPTING TO NEW CONSUMER EXPECTATIONS AND BEHAVIOR PATTERNS

The landscape of consumer behavior is evolving rapidly, driven by technological advancements, shifting cultural norms, and emerging trends. Marketers must stay attuned to these changes to effectively engage with their audiences and meet new expectations. Here's how consumer behavior is changing and how you can adapt your marketing strategies accordingly:

1. Increasing Demand for Personalization

Overview: Consumers now expect highly personalized experiences tailored to their individual preferences and behaviors. This shift is driven by advancements in data analytics and AI, which enable brands to deliver more relevant content and recommendations.

Adaptation Strategies:

- **Leverage Data Analytics**: Use data to gain insights into customer preferences, behaviors, and interactions. Implement AI-driven tools to create personalized recommendations, offers, and content.

- **Segment Your Audience**: Develop detailed customer segments and personas based on data. Tailor your messaging and marketing strategies to address the specific needs and preferences of each segment.

- **Implement Personalization Across Channels**: Ensure that personalization extends across all touchpoints, including email, social media, and website interactions. Consistent, personalized experiences enhance customer satisfaction and loyalty.

2. Growing Focus on Ethical and Sustainable Practices

Overview: Consumers are increasingly concerned with ethical and environmental issues, seeking brands that demonstrate social responsibility and sustainable practices. This trend reflects a broader shift towards values-driven consumption.

Adaptation Strategies:

- **Communicate Your Values**: Clearly articulate your brand's commitment to ethical practices and sustainability. Highlight initiatives, such as eco-friendly products, ethical sourcing, or charitable contributions, in your marketing efforts.

- **Transparency and Authenticity**: Be transparent about your practices and supply chain. Consumers value authenticity and are more likely to support brands that are open about their operations and impact.

- **Incorporate Sustainable Practices**: Integrate sustainability into your product development, packaging, and overall business operations. Promote these practices as part of your brand's identity and messaging.

3. Rise of Omnichannel Experiences

Overview: Consumers now interact with brands across multiple channels and devices, expecting a seamless and integrated experience. Omnichannel strategies ensure consistency and continuity throughout the customer journey.

Adaptation Strategies:

- **Integrate Channels**: Develop a cohesive omnichannel strategy that integrates online and offline channels. Ensure that customer experiences are consistent, whether interacting through social media, email, mobile apps, or physical stores.

- **Utilize Cross-Channel Data**: Collect and analyze data from all customer touchpoints to gain a holistic view of interactions and preferences. Use this data to optimize and personalize cross-channel experiences.

- **Enhance Mobile Experiences**: Given the increasing use of mobile devices, ensure that your mobile app and website offer a seamless and user-friendly experience. Implement responsive design and optimize for fast loading times.

4. Expectation for Instant Gratification

Overview: The rise of digital technology has heightened consumers' expectations for immediate responses and instant access to information and services. This shift impacts how they engage with brands and make purchasing decisions.

Adaptation Strategies:

- **Streamline Processes**: Simplify and expedite processes such as purchasing, customer service, and information retrieval. Implement features like one-click purchasing, chatbots for instant support, and fast-loading content.

- **Prioritize Speed and Efficiency**: Ensure that your website, app, and customer service channels are optimized for speed and efficiency. Quick response times and easy navigation enhance the overall customer experience.

- **Offer Real-Time Interaction**: Leverage technologies such as live chat and social media to provide real-time engagement with customers. Address inquiries and issues promptly to meet the demand for instant gratification.

5. Emphasis on Authentic and User-Generated Content

Overview: Consumers increasingly value authentic, user-generated content (UGC) over traditional advertising. UGC, such as reviews, testimonials, and social media posts, is perceived as more trustworthy and relatable.

Adaptation Strategies:

- **Encourage UGC**: Foster and encourage user-generated content by creating opportunities for customers to share their experiences and opinions. Run campaigns that invite customers to submit reviews, photos, or videos related to your brand.

- **Leverage Social Proof**: Showcase UGC on your website, social media, and marketing materials. Highlight positive reviews and testimonials to build credibility and trust with potential customers.

- **Engage with Your Community**: Actively engage with your audience on social media and other platforms. Respond to UGC, participate in conversations, and show appreciation for customer contributions.

6. Growing Use of Voice Search and Smart Devices

Overview: The proliferation of voice-activated devices and smart technology is changing how consumers search for information and interact with brands. Voice search and smart devices are becoming integral parts of daily life.

Adaptation Strategies:

- **Optimize for Voice Search**: Adapt your SEO strategy to include voice search optimization. Focus on natural language keywords and question-based queries that align with how users speak.

- **Develop Voice-Activated Features**: Explore opportunities to integrate voice-activated features into your products or services. Consider creating voice apps or skills that enhance user interaction with your brand.

- **Monitor Smart Device Trends**: Stay informed about trends in smart devices and their impact on consumer behavior. Adapt your marketing strategies to align with emerging technologies and user preferences.

By understanding and adapting to these changing consumer behaviors, marketers can develop more effective strategies that meet evolving expectations and drive better engagement. Staying ahead of these trends will ensure that your campaigns remain relevant and impactful in a dynamic marketplace.

SUSTAINABLE AND ETHICAL MARKETING: EMBRACING SUSTAINABILITY AND ETHICS IN MARKETING PRACTICES

In an era where consumers are increasingly aware of environmental and social issues, integrating sustainability and ethics into marketing practices is not just a trend—it's a necessity. Brands that embrace these principles not only enhance their reputation but also build stronger, more authentic connections with their audience. Here's how to effectively incorporate sustainability and ethical practices into your marketing strategies:

1. Align with Core Values

Overview: Sustainable and ethical marketing starts with a strong alignment between a brand's values and its actions. This alignment ensures that marketing efforts are genuine and reflect the brand's commitment to positive practices.

Implementation Strategies:

- **Define Your Values**: Clearly articulate your brand's commitment to sustainability and ethics. Ensure these values are embedded in your mission statement, business practices, and marketing messages.

- **Communicate Authentically**: Use transparent and honest messaging to convey your commitment to ethical and sustainable practices. Avoid greenwashing—make sure your claims are backed by real, measurable actions.

2. Implement Sustainable Practices

Overview: Sustainability involves adopting practices that minimize environmental impact and promote long-term ecological health. This can influence various aspects of your marketing, from product development to promotional materials.

Implementation Strategies:

- **Eco-Friendly Products**: Offer products that are designed with sustainability in mind, such as those made from recycled materials, renewable resources, or with minimal packaging. Highlight these aspects in your marketing campaigns.

- **Sustainable Packaging**: Use eco-friendly packaging options, such as biodegradable or recyclable materials. Communicate your packaging choices to consumers to emphasize your commitment to reducing waste.

- **Green Supply Chain**: Ensure that your supply chain adheres to sustainable practices. Partner with suppliers who share your values and are committed to ethical and environmentally friendly operations.

3. Promote Ethical Practices

Overview: Ethical marketing involves ensuring that your marketing practices are fair, honest, and respectful of consumer rights. This includes avoiding deceptive practices and promoting inclusivity and diversity.

Implementation Strategies:

- **Transparency**: Be open about your marketing practices, pricing, and product information. Provide clear and accurate information to help consumers make informed decisions.

- **Inclusive Messaging**: Create marketing content that reflects diversity and promotes inclusivity. Avoid stereotypes and ensure that your messaging is respectful and representative of different groups.

- **Ethical Advertising**: Avoid manipulative or deceptive advertising tactics. Ensure that your claims are substantiated and that your advertisements do not exploit vulnerable populations.

4. Engage with the Community

Overview: Engaging with the community involves supporting local initiatives and fostering positive relationships with consumers and stakeholders. This can enhance your brand's reputation and demonstrate a genuine commitment to social responsibility.

Implementation Strategies:

- **Support Local Causes**: Partner with local organizations and contribute to community projects or charitable causes. Highlight these partnerships in your marketing to show your brand's involvement in positive social impact.

- **Encourage Consumer Participation**: Involve consumers in sustainability efforts, such as recycling programs or community clean-up events. Create campaigns that encourage participation and demonstrate the collective impact of these efforts.

- **Build Partnerships**: Collaborate with other brands, non-profits, or influencers who share your commitment to sustainability and ethics. Joint initiatives can amplify your message and reach a broader audience.

5. Measure and Report Impact

Overview: To build credibility and trust, it's essential to measure and report the impact of your sustainability and ethical initiatives. This demonstrates accountability and allows consumers to see the tangible results of your efforts.

Implementation Strategies:

- **Track Performance**: Use metrics and KPIs to measure the effectiveness of your sustainability and ethical practices. Monitor progress and assess the impact of your initiatives on both the environment and community.

- **Report Transparently**: Share your results with consumers and stakeholders through reports, infographics, or case studies. Highlight successes and areas for improvement to demonstrate ongoing commitment.

- **Seek Feedback**: Collect feedback from consumers and stakeholders to understand their perceptions of your sustainability and ethical practices. Use this feedback to refine your strategies and enhance your efforts.

6. Innovate and Lead

Overview: Embracing sustainability and ethics often involves leading the way with innovative solutions and setting new industry standards. Brands that take a proactive approach can differentiate themselves and inspire others to follow.

Implementation Strategies:

- **Explore New Technologies**: Investigate emerging technologies and practices that enhance sustainability and ethical marketing. Stay ahead of trends and be open to adopting new solutions that align with your values.

- **Set Industry Standards**: Aim to set benchmarks for sustainability and ethical practices within your industry. Advocate for positive change and inspire other brands to follow suit.

Incorporating sustainability and ethics into your marketing practices not only meets the growing consumer demand for responsible business practices but also fosters long-term success and brand loyalty. By aligning your marketing strategies with these principles, you can build a brand that stands out for its commitment to positive impact and social responsibility.

EMBRACING MODERN MARKETING PRACTICES

This book has provided a comprehensive exploration of modern marketing, offering insights into effective campaign strategies, emerging technologies, and ethical practices. It serves as a fundamental guide to navigating the complexities of today's marketing landscape, equipped with the knowledge needed to develop and execute impactful campaigns.

However, understanding the principles outlined here is just the beginning. To truly excel in marketing, it is essential to implement these tactics with precision and adaptability. The real value lies in applying these strategies in your unique context, continuously experimenting, and refining your approach based on real-world results.

Stay curious and vigilant about emerging marketing trends and technological advancements. The marketing field is dynamic, with new tools, platforms, and consumer behaviors constantly evolving. Embrace the opportunity to learn and adapt, leveraging the latest innovations to stay ahead of the curve.

Most importantly, be willing to try new things. Innovation often comes from experimentation and a willingness to step outside of conventional approaches. By staying open to new ideas and continuously refining your strategies, you will not only enhance your marketing efforts but also position yourself as a leader in an ever-changing industry.

The journey to marketing excellence is ongoing, and this book is your starting point. Use it as a foundation to build upon, explore new horizons, and drive success in your marketing endeavors.

FROM TRUEFUTURE MEDIA

As you embark on your journey to mastering modern marketing, remember that TrueFuture Media is here to support you every step of the way. Our team of experts specializes in creating tailored marketing strategies, leveraging cutting-edge technologies, and delivering results-driven campaigns. Whether you need guidance on implementing these tactics or want to explore innovative approaches, TrueFuture Media is dedicated to helping your business thrive in the digital age. Connect with us at **TrueFutureMedia.com** to elevate your marketing efforts and achieve your goals with precision and creativity.

INDEX

www.ingramcontent.com/pod-product-compliance
Lightning Source LLC
Chambersburg PA
CBHW071831210526
45479CB00001B/87